THE COLOR OF YOUR DREAMS

PUBLISH YOUR DAMN BOOK ALREADY

DOM TESTA

PROFOUND IMPACT GROUP, LLC

Books may be purchased in quantity by contacting the publisher
directly:
Profound Impact Group, LLC
P.O. Box 506
Alpharetta, GA 30009
Info@ProfoundGroup.com

ISBN: 978-1-942151-19-7 (Print)
978-1-942151-20-3 (ebook)

Cover design: 100 Covers

ALSO BY DOM TESTA

Writing As Buster Blank

Shaking Demons

Madison Cooley's Shoes

My Favorite Nightmare

Writing As Harlan Plumber

Wednesday, and Other Dark Tales

CONTENTS

INTRODUCTION

When my father passed away, my siblings and I found a large box tucked into the back of his bedroom closet. Inside he'd squirreled away all sorts of memorabilia, ranging from newspaper clippings to crinkled photos to lottery tickets. Losing tickets, of course.

Near the bottom of the box my sister retrieved a red spiral notebook. It turned out to be the English composition notebook from my third grade class at the American school in Verona, Italy. My eight-year-old self had scrawled the name "Dominic Testa" across the top of the cover in very respectable cursive, thank you.

And inside? A veritable treasure trove of essays, accompanied by the author's crayon illustrations. Among the titles:

- *A Field Trip* (where our class saw Juliet's balcony, as in "*Romeo, Romeo*")
- *My Favorite Pet* (up to that point my *only* pet, actually, a German Shepherd named Tiber)

- *Looking for Fossils* (which, I guess, could've been *A Field Trip, Part Two*)

But the winner, without a doubt, written in early December that year, was called *My Boring Family*. Apparently my parents and my sister were frightfully busy and unable to entertain me around the clock, so that shit got catalogued for posterity.

Thus began a career based on words. Spanning many decades, I've now been paid to speak words on stage and on the radio and paid to scribble words between the covers of books.

Money from words. I'm sure at your core you know it's possible, and you've dreamed it could happen to you. But there are a few things holding you back, preventing you from jumping in, paralyzing you. One big thing in particular.

Which we'll get to in a moment. In fact, we'll make it the entire focus of the next chapter. For now, though, let's see if I can paint an accurate portrait of you.

You enjoy reading and likely always have. You keep several books beside your bed, either because you're one of those people who's able to keep more than one going at a time or because your book queue is longer than your Netflix queue. *There's so much to read!*

When you read, you often find yourself thinking, *This doesn't seem that hard. I could do better than this.*

You've started writing—and subsequently stopped writing—several books or at least stories. The ideas got you excited, but then you ran out of steam. Or got distracted. Or discouraged. You may or may not have these stories hidden away.

You've at least glanced at a book on writing, maybe Anne Lamott's or Stephen King's or one of the older classics. (And if you haven't picked those up, please do so.) There's a good chance you've devoured these and others completely. They got you fired up for a few days or weeks, and then you lost the spark.

You've told hardly anyone that you want to write a book, because it's somehow embarrassing. But you *do* want to.

You're looking at this book for several—or all—of the reasons above.

It's time to quit screwing around and get with the program.

Of course, I'm a big talker. I lugged around the dream of professional writing (professional = paid) for almost twenty years and never did squat to make it happen. Yes, I wrote some short stories—pretty good ones, too—and kept them in a drawer. I think I submitted one piece to a newspaper, their *Let's Hear From the Readers!* section, never heard a peep from them, and interpreted that to mean I should never write another word.

So I focused on the radio portion of my life. Hey, that's been successful, so no complaints there. But those were valuable years where I could've built up a reservoir of stories, essays, and novels. My old word processor (remember those?) gathered dust.

Until one day it didn't, and I got reacquainted with my

secret love affair with words. They spilled out, eventually forming a 65,000-word young adult novel.

Before I could talk myself out of it, I self-published the book, years before it was cool to do that on your own. And some funny things happened. I'll spare you the details until they're needed for specific chapters of this book, but the bottom line was a six-book contract from a major New York publisher.

Moral of the story: Waiting is idiotic.

This book will not teach you how to write. These pages are not about the art of storytelling, nor how to craft a perfect paragraph. I have enough experience to attempt that, and perhaps I'm as qualified as other authors, but there's no schooling I could give you that would be any better than countless existing volumes on the subject.

No, this isn't a book on *how* to write. It's a book about getting off your ass. It's about the reasons you've ignored your creative urges, and how you can stop ignoring them.

And it's mostly about what to do once you get serious about stringing words together.

Yes, that means publishing them. I'm going to prepare you to be published, even if you're kicking and screaming along the way. I'm targeting your spirit.

I'm not going to give you any bullshit speech about how the world needs your writing. Regardless of what flowery instructors say and what you've seen on social media memes, the world doesn't need your writing. Or *anybody's* writing, for that matter. It's already got plenty. Have you *seen* the shelves at bookstores? Have you scanned the *millions* of titles online? You really think the world needs your words?

F the world, as we say. This isn't about the freakin' world. This is about you and your voice. Whether one million people read your work or just one person, you need to get your words out there for *you*. *You* need your words.

And while we're at it, let's dispense with this nonsense that you're somehow not qualified to write, that you need an MFA from some prestigious university or a journalism degree or some other pedigree. You don't.

What you *do* need is something to say. Something interesting, unique, fun, funny, compelling, educational, tear-inducing, inspiring, or any combination of the above. You need a clear understanding of how to transfer your vision into print. You need the resolve to stick to it until you see your name on a cover.

Writers, by their nature, are insecure as hell. In this book we'll attack that problem and beat it into submission. I titled this book *The Color of Your Dreams* because I am and will always be an admirer of John Lennon. In his song *Tomorrow Never Knows*, he urged us to listen to the color of our dreams. That imagery has moved me since I was young.

You and I have dreams to write and publish, and each of our dreams has its own color. And within those colors you'll likely identify countless shades of each. It's time for you to explore them, and it's definitely time for you to listen to them. They have a lot to say to you.

You'll notice this isn't a large book. It doesn't have to be. It has just the right amount of information and inspiration you need to stop crawling and to start running. Just keep in mind that you could spend the rest of your life *reading* about writing, but eventually you have to write. More on that later.

From humble essays in a red grade-school notebook to more than twenty published manuscripts, I'm qualified to help you on this path because I was handcuffed by the same damned thing that's stifling you. And it's the subject of the next chapter.

Fear. Stupid, baseless, insidious fear.

Let's get to it.

1

FEAR

I'm afraid of spiders and Steve Buscemi.

He's a terrific actor and deserves every accolade he receives, I'm sure. But for some reason I have a strange reaction when he comes on screen, and I finally decided that I'm just afraid of him. It makes no sense, but there it is.

The fear of spiders is baseless, too. Some people have childhood stories of giant, hairy spiders dropping into their lap or crawling under their sheets one night. I see how that could traumatize anyone. I don't have a story like that. As far as I know I've never been bitten by one, and unless you count panic-filled dreams where they've invaded my bed—I've actually awakened and torn off all the covers in search of them—the little bastards have never molested me.

But I'm afraid of them. Not "jump up on a chair and scream" fear, but a shuddering dislike, nonetheless. Seriously, I've often considered moving to Arizona for its climate, but have ultimately resisted because I don't want tarantulas (or scorpions, another member of the arachnid family) in my house.

FEAR IS FASCINATING. If we're to believe scientists, many of our fears are rooted in evolution. Since a lot of people share my dread of eight-legged monsters, it's reasonable to think that spiders must've jacked with our ancestors big time. Over the millennia that transitioned into an inborn fear of spiders. Same with other critters, like snakes or things with sharp fangs. I get it.

But now explain our fear of letting strangers read our writing. What, did some caveman get all butt-hurt over a one-star review of his cave chronicles? Good ol' *Homo erectus* came up with the hand ax and other cool stone tools, but he never got within 100,000 years of writing a memoir. Soiling yourself over a saber-toothed tiger is understandable. Being afraid of writing makes no sense.

And yet there it is. The fear lies simmering inside every writer. The ones who say they're fearless are trying to impress you, but they're liars.

The question is: Why? Why are we afraid? And what is it exactly that creates fear in even the most successful authors? Is it the writing itself? The act of composing? Are we stressed out over the creative process?

No. It's not the *act* of writing that concerns us (although many seasoned writers will tell you they don't really like writing; they like *the results* of writing, the finished product).

It's the reception. In other words, we fear the response of readers.

Again, it makes no sense. Like the poor, innocent spiders that have never come within miles of us, we'll never see 99% percent of the people who flip through the pages of our work. We won't know their names, what they look like, where they live, their hygiene practices, nothing.

And yet they have the power to scare us through the simple act of perusing our product. It's almost identical to the fear associated with public speaking. Standing up alone in a room? No problem. But plop one hundred strangers in chairs, facing you, awaiting your words? For most people trembling sets in, the mind goes foggy, the sweat glands go into overdrive, and the words either don't come or they come in a nervous wash.

(Side note: This is one of the reasons some of us make pretty good coin with public speaking. People often are willing to pay well for something they themselves would hate to do. I talked with a guy who cleans residential septic systems and he makes a killing because few people want to suck out shit for a living.)

So, for creative people, it's not the activity that terrifies. It explains why millions of people have dozens of stories or half-finished manuscripts lying around. Writing the words is easy—well, comparatively speaking. But showing those words to people, especially strangers, creates a panic attack.

And it's not just a fear that someone will think the words are awful. I sat on several stories for years because I simply didn't believe anyone would find them *interesting*. Then I published them and immediately received enthusiastic feedback.

Well, shit. Why did I sit on the damned things for so long? Because I'd read, re-read, and then re-read the stories so many times during writing and editing that they became stale and boring in *my* mind. But new readers were into them. And I have to admit, when I dug them out after ages in a file, they were fresh and interesting to me again, too. Honestly, I'd forgotten how one of them ended. You have no idea how funny it is to be surprised by a story that *you* wrote.

WE WORRY that people will either harshly judge our words or just be bored by them—which, to me, is worse. And this anxiety creates a paralysis. The next thing you know, the words you labored over for weeks or months— or years—wind up hidden away in a file, and the only evidence we have that you're a writer is your pronouncement.

So what's the answer? Believe it or not, the age of online commenting actually helps. This sounds counterintuitive. You'd think a flood of people popping off about your writing makes it even more frightening, but the opposite is true.

Stay with me, here. It'll make sense.

In the days before the web, book reviews and literary criticism were mostly reserved for the pros, or for whatever passed as professional. The critics for the *New York Times,* for example, were deemed experts in the ways of the written word, and their blessing or condemnation of a book spoke for us all, whether we liked it or not. Outside of newspapers and magazines, there really weren't outlets for reviews. And that meant one bad review and you were screwed.

Sometimes I wonder how many fantastic books never got a real chance at success because the *Times* reviewer had fought with his wife that morning.

I've imagined writers in those days, sitting by the phone, waiting for a call from their agent, who would relay the news from the eight or ten primary critics. Their opinions were paramount. Talk about pressure.

Now consider the situation today. You release a book, and those same oh-so-important critics will spout off about it.

But this is critical: So will hundreds or thousands of other people. And, guaranteed, you'll have people who hate your words and people who adore your words. You just will. Wanna know how I know? Take any book you like—*any* book—and go check out the online reviews. *To Kill A Mockingbird*, for example. Considered by many to be one of the top three greatest American novels ever. And it has more one-star reviews than you can imagine. That's right, there are people who call *TKAM* shit.

(Although, granted, one of those one-star reviews was —if you'll pardon the pun—a lark. The guy simply wanted to point out that the book never actually showed you how to kill the damned bird. Kudos to that sarcastic bastard.)

And why is this good news for you? Because it alleviates the pressure. Suddenly you understand that the months and months of work you pour into your novel

5

won't matter to some people, and they'll trash your words regardless of what others think.

In other words, you're gonna get ripped by some idiot out there. But Grisham, Rowling, King, Tolkien, Angelou, Faulkner, and even Seuss get shredded by someone. According to some accounts, Agatha Christie has sold more than a *billion* books, and yet there are legions of people who say her writing sucked. Sigh.

If you're hung up on the reception of your words, you have to step back and recognize that we've entered an age where everyone is encouraged to comment on everything. On top of that, there are trolls in basements who are frustrated that *their* book wasn't a hit and so they're out for blood. You might just make a convenient target.

My books have received good, medium, and bad reviews. That's because *every* book receives good, medium, and bad reviews. You're only interested, though, in the people who *enjoy* your words, and you'll write your next book for them. Trust me, they'll eagerly await it.

FEAR OF ACCEPTANCE is a natural pathology. People want to be liked, and that certainly extends to their creative side. Painters love it if gallery visitors rave about their canvas. Singers long to sell lots of records. Actors lust for the gold statue. But award-winners also receive their share of raspberries.

Don't let your fear of the public's reception to your work prevent you from getting it out there. If only a handful of people determined your fate, it would be intimidating. When millions of people sound off, it suddenly becomes background noise.

Put your head down, crank out your words, and say what you want to say without worrying about critics. You're a writer because there's something you want to say or a story you want to tell. We don't write for reviewers. We write because we *want* to.

2

DISTRACTION

B lame the Internet. That's what everyone else does.

I'm talking about the reason you don't get your writing done, and, consequently, why your words don't end up in print. Same with all of the poor little gadgets, like the cell phone or the tablet or the video game. They're consistently accused of sabotaging the efforts of writers.

In a seemingly never-ending quest to overcome these abominable tools of convenience, we search for help, ironically from other electronic marvels. Digital task programs. Calendar overlords. Project management systems. Hell, there are apps you can download to your phone or laptop that lock out the Internet for a prescribed length of time, just so you can get your work finished.

Yes, we're at the point where our own willpower and determination be damned. We can't cut it. We need digital supervisors to shepherd our efforts and keep us focused.

Distraction is easily blamed on outside influences, and these do contribute quite a bit. I readily admit to working better away from home because the lure of things—even stupid, mindless things—is too great around the house. It's as if we need to have something evil to act as scapegoat for our own shortcomings. *I can't help it! Those email alerts keep going off.*

Which is patently ridiculous, and we *know* it's ridiculous, but it's an odd compact we've made with the Muse or whatever label you assign to your creative side: *I'll humor you occasionally with five hundred words, but I reserve the right to screw around whenever I like and it won't be my fault. Do you hear me? Not. My. Fault.*

We're all wired differently when it comes to outside distractions. For writers, a prime example is the cliched coffee shop. I saw a comic strip about a guy who innocently sat alone in a coffee shop with no laptop and no cell phone to stare at. Just sat there, drinking his coffee and looking around. *What a weirdo*, one woman thinks to herself before diving back into her little screen.

It *is* kinda funny that generally people on their laptops outnumber the people just sitting there or chatting with another humanoid. It's a sign of the times when the most-frequent complaint baristas receive has nothing to do with the beverages and everything to do with the number of available outlets.

But coffee shops don't work for everyone. I really *want* to write there, but the conversation at the table next to me is just too interesting or the music is bothersome. I understand that some people need that background ambiance. I mean, there's even an app for that, too. Yes, a "sounds of the coffee shop" app in case you're stuck at home and need that clinky/chatty/dark-roasted atmosphere in order to spew words.

There's a fine line, however, between something that distracts versus something that provides respite.

For instance, I heard a podcast interview with writer Nick Hornby (*High Fidelity, About a Boy,* and the screenplay for Cheryl Strayed's *Wild*). He mentioned keeping a jigsaw puzzle going at a table beside his writing workspace and how he'll sometimes turn around and labor over it.

As someone who's been a jigsaw freak since childhood—and has assembled a 24,000-piece behemoth—I was instantly intrigued. I wondered if this was a trick I could borrow, then just as quickly discarded the idea. Nick is able to use it to clear his mind for additional writing, but I know myself. I would get lost in the puzzle and maybe not resurface for days.

Paraphrasing a Clint Eastwood character, *"We've all got to know our limitations."* What may be a therapeutic break for you could be a subversive distraction for me.

Then there are the necessary outside distractions, the kinds you can't just ignore. Although it may be the ultimate dream, you're likely not able to write full-time yet and so this thing called "a job" pops up. If you're in a relationship, you better figure out a way to wedge your writing life into *that* commitment. We have obligations and responsibilities. We gotta pay the bills and we gotta keep our people happy.

Oh, and don't forget parenting. It's probably disrespectful to label that a distraction, but can we agree it's vexing trying to pen a bestseller when some little—but loud—person is demanding a goddamned peanut butter sandwich?

So yeah, there are real life distractions, and there's nothing you can do about most of those.

What really interests me, though, are not necessarily the outside distractions, but the inner. To me, cell phones and video games and family are nothing compared to our own, self-inflicted damage. The kind you can't blame on anything else.

We already touched on fear, which is, as we described it, internally generated. But in its purest sense, a distraction is, quoting one dictionary source, "*that which divides the attention or prevents concentration.*"

Based on that definition, I nominate, as the worst offender in the writer's pantheon of distraction, the syndrome I call "the new baby in the house."

Here's an example. Like you, I have ideas for stories or articles spring to mind that immediately captivate me. I'll jot down notes and even some narrative or dialogue, things I'm sure will propel the idea into a published smash hit. It's not unusual for the first chapter or two to spill out, my fingers barely able to keep up with the word flow. It's gonna be huge.

And then . . .

And then another idea strikes me. An idea just as tantalizing, maybe more so. And I jot down notes and even some narrative or dialogue. A first chapter may even materialize.

At this point you're saying, "*Wait, what about the first idea?*"

It's been abandoned. Maybe not officially. You still keep the manuscript on your desktop, or simply minimized in the lower task bar. But c'mon, the new baby in the house—that fresh story idea, the one that promises publishing superstardom—has kidnapped your attention.

Now that I think of it, perhaps the new-baby metaphor isn't right. This is more like a siren song, the pernicious call leading you to paralyzing doom. Paralyzing because you'll get two or three chapters into this new idea before yet another steals your soul. Sidetrack after sidetrack.

See, this is an all-too-real form of distraction that doesn't get the attention normally paid to tangible, physical things like phones and email. And I believe, at its core, it's more damaging. We can lock up our phones and shut off the Internet connection, but we can't shut off our monkey minds. There's no downloadable app to lock up your brain and keep it on task.

I'd pay $99 for one if it existed. Maybe more. Probably more.

If you're looking for the cheap and easy solution to this problem, I'm afraid you won't find one. This is where pure discipline is required, the only tonic that can help. You need to cultivate a mental toughness to catalogue new ideas, including a few quick notes, and then put the idea down for a nap. It'll still be there when you finish the first project.

· · ·

AND THEN WE get to the internal distraction created by fantasy. No, not the dragon, wizard, troll, or gorgon forms of fantasy, but rather the dreams we concoct about the eventual success of our words.

Everyone will love this! Easily number one on Amazon. New York will come calling with a seven-figure contract for all the follow-ups. I want the new house on a lake somewhere, with a dock. Oh, and a little kitchenette in my master bedroom.

You know, the stuff we incessantly think about when we should actually be producing the words that would generate the fantasy life we're imagining.

To be fair, a bit of fantasy is not only okay, but it's also an important ingredient to success. After all, we're told we need to visualize success, right? It's why people create vision boards.

The problem comes when we slip headlong into a dream world, and we spend all our time visualizing rather than creating. Just like your diet, a healthy mix is crucial. And don't ask, "*What's a healthy mix?*" You're bullshitting yourself if you pretend to not know where the line is drawn.

No need to feel guilty if you've occupied Fantasy Land for too long. Today is a good day to put your fantasy life on its own diet. It's a distraction when it's bloated, and our goal is to minimize distractions.

SO WE'VE SEEN the enemy, and it is distraction. Some are external, many are internal, and all of them are threats to the fragile framework of creation. Don't beat yourself up over a few random detours along your path. Just pay attention to what is most often hijacking your time and figure out a plan that helps to protect those valuable minutes. It could be as simple as finding an isolated, quiet oasis where you can paint a picture with your words.

We'll explore that specific strategy in the next chapter. In the meantime, stay committed and true to the color of your dreams. Just don't get lost in the palette.

3

SOLITUDE

This brief chapter is more like a subchapter to the previous topic of distraction. For a few moments I'd like for you to consider the gift of solitude.

Because that's really what it is: a gift, a blessing. Most of us live in a maelstrom of noise and people. We sit in traffic, we work in an office full of chatter, our neighborhood is teeming with families of excitable children. Even our own home, our nest, may be occupied by two or three or more other bodies.

Sure, we love them. (Yes, you do. Stop grimacing, and repeat: "*I made this choice. I made this choice. I made this choice.*") But you need to get away, and getting away from it all requires effort.

Granted, ten different writers might have ten different environments that best stimulate their creativity and/or productivity. (Both, by the way, are necessary for success. You can be creative in your head all day long, but if you're not productive in transferring the ideas from your brain cells to a keyboard, what's the point?)

Of all the possibilities, you likely have found one that works for you. Or you think it does, anyway. Those who can write in the midst of a human storm, such as a coffee shop or crowded park or loud household, impress me. That might be you.

It's possible, however, that you're missing out on a chance to truly grow as an artist. Being alone—really alone, not just sitting at a table by yourself in the middle of a jammed cafe—could work wonders for you. It could open pathways that were shrouded by stimulation.

I'm convinced that real creativity demands solitude. As legendary inventor/genius Nikola Tesla said, "*Be alone. That is the secret of invention. Be alone. That is when ideas are born.*"

It's not something we cultivate today. Far from it, in fact. From a young age students are herded together to come up with solutions to problems, when in fact they could each be supplied the facts and then sent off on their own to work it out.

The same concept applies to so-called brainstorming sessions at work. I cringe when I get an email announcing a mandatory brainstorming meeting. What any notice like that should say is, "*Please join our group as we stare at each other and accomplish little.*"

Maybe there have been some great ideas that have sprung from these sessions, and there likely are constructive ways to collectively dream up a winner. But I'm an advocate for getting away from the group in order to truly stimulate creativity.

Corporate managers fear the lone wolf in their fold, and I wish that wasn't so. A team of lone wolves might not gather as a group often, but I'll bet when they do it's a helluva lot more productive than weekly brainstorming sessions.

Why not just describe the problem to attack, and then have everyone come to a meeting after they've each come up with a solution?

NOW CONSIDER creative writing and other artistic endeavors. Group lessons and well-planned workshops serve an important purpose, and it's a good idea to experience them. But afterward, get away. Far away. A mind flourishes when left to its own devices. If you're serious about your growth as a writer, the best thing you can do is demand alone time.

That means submerging into your thoughts and providing a growth medium for your subconscious, without outside stimuli. I enjoy socializing with my friends as much as anyone, but when it's time to write, you won't find another soul in my house. Or I take off for someplace that guarantees no other souls around.

"WITHOUT GREAT SOLITUDE *no serious work is possible.*" Those are the words of Picasso, who knew a thing or two about creativity.

Sadly, the concept of solitude is disappearing for many people. Being truly alone has become alien. Companionship is always just a text or tweet away. Society even stigmatizes people who want to be by themselves. Hermits, or those lone wolves, get a bad rap, and we often equate being alone with loneliness and sadness.

But that's not right. Some of the most brilliant, creative minds we've ever known made their discoveries or rolled out their masterpieces when they were secluded. As Albert Einstein pointed out, "*I take time to go for long walks on the beach so that I can listen to what is going on inside my head.*"

You don't need a beach, though. You simply need to find a quiet place in order to stir the ingredients for great ideas.

Creativity sparkles when the outside world is sealed off. Don't fear it. Seek it out.

4

WORDS

Yesterday, working for a little over an hour, I produced 644 words. Good words, too. It was a fulfilling day of writing, because I enjoyed the content.

Exactly a week earlier I'd produced 1,202 words for the day. Now, on the surface you could say that was a more-productive session than yesterday's, and I suppose it technically was. I mean, twice the output has to be better, right?

Except I wasn't as jazzed about the content from the earlier session. Not bad, just not as enjoyable as yesterday's bounty.

After thinking about this for a while I came to the conclusion that our scorecard is based on the wrong unit of measurement.

We need to have a come-to-Jesus meeting about word counts. I can't understand why so many people—including writing instructors—get bogged down with word counts. "*Set a goal, and sit there as long as it takes to hit that goal*," they'll say.

Well, okay. Then what? Pat yourself on the back and go grab a Snickers?

For the record, if you have a word-count goal each day or each week, cool. I'm not here to talk you out of it. In fact, I hope you reach it. But let's look at this a different way, and maybe it'll bring you a bit of peace.

I'm suspicious of word counts. For a long time I subscribed to the goal theory and found myself settling on something like 1,200 words a day. That was the magic number. Why? Damned if I know. Just sounded do-able and would produce 400,000 words in a calendar year, assuming thirty days of inactivity.

You know what happened? I never kept track of my daily word count for longer than two or three weeks. Then, a few months later, I'd vow to once again religiously monitor it. And that vow would be forgotten in another fortnight.

The problem, as I see it, lies in this belief that setting a word-count goal will somehow keep us disciplined and on track. And for some people it definitely will. Bully for them, and for you, if you're in that group. It's possible that dedicating yourself to a specific target will, ultimately, develop a disciplined mindset that you'll be able to exploit for years to come. I get it.

But we're aiming for consistent, quality work, not some arbitrary number of words. There are days when I'll crank out a bunch, days when I'll do nothing, and days where I feel great about one paragraph or even just one little outline.

I eventually found that setting 1,200 words—or 2500,

or 350—as a finish line did a couple of things that could jack with my head. Any writer's head.

For one thing, suppose you're determined to bang out 1,000 words a day, and, after a couple of hours or so, you're out of gas but sitting at 519. So you force yourself to sit there and spew some garbage until the little digital counter at the bottom of the page says 1,009, and you (sorta) feel satisfied.

Then, later, you read your work and realize you were simply chasing a number, not an idea or a plot. You sacrificed your story or your article in order to meet some arbitrary number. Sure, you could go back later and rewrite it. But that only makes the original session even more pointless to me.

Or, here's a different scenario that may be just as bad. You can't do any more that day, so you shut down your laptop at the 519-word mark and binge-watch that show with Reese Witherspoon. Then, later, you feel like shit because you failed to keep your word about the words. So, naturally, you then temporarily install a new goal of 1,500 to make up for your half-assed day, and you experience one of these same two outcomes.

To me, there are two ultimate goals that don't necessarily require hitting any premeditated word count. One is producing work that's good, work that you feel others will enjoy. The other is producing a feeling of contentment within yourself that will bring you back to the blinking cursor the next day. If we're going to commit ourselves to the craft, we need to like it. A lot. If we feel like we're failing—and for reasons that have nothing to do with the quality of the words—we'll begin to resent it, even if subconsciously. We'll avoid sitting at the keyboard. And that's a damned shame.

(It's no different than exercising when your heart's not in it. Why do you think so many people storm the gym on January 2nd and disappear by the 29th? They want to get in shape but they don't love the process. In fact, they probably hate it.)

If you commit yourself to simply writing, without the arbitrary number, you'll have days of great big honkin' word counts and days where that cursor barely moves. Sure, you can average those out if you *must* have a number. I'm OCD, too, by the way, but about other things, so I feel ya.

Placing a strict rule on your creative output, especially at an early stage of your writing career, takes the emphasis off your quality of words and puts it on math. *Okay, just 340 more words. Now 325. Ooh, only 309 left.*

The key is consistency, not numbers. And by consistency I mean getting into a habit of producing words. I think you'll find the more you do it the more you'll want to do it, especially if there's not some grim reaper dude hanging out next to your writing station, eyeballing your word count and sharpening his scythe. (It is a scythe, right?)

If you're going to make money from your writing, whether it's a fortune or just walkin'-around money, it should be something you truly enjoy doing. Otherwise it's just another clock-punching job, where an obligation sucks the fun right out of it. We don't want that.

So the appropriate unit of measurement isn't the number of words, but how you honestly feel about the day's work. Honesty being the key word. If you get up from a session and feel like you hit it out of the park, nobody should give a rat's ass how many words that constituted. Two hundred? Two thousand? I don't know. Were they *great* words?

THIS ISN'T an excuse to blow off your work, by the way. *Hooray! Dom says I don't have to keep track of my words! Let's go to the pool!* If you go six months and produce 900 words total, then maybe this life isn't for you.

But people who are serious about making a career from their words know they can do it *and* enjoy the process.

Let's keep it fun and uplifting, okay?

(For what it's worth, working on this chapter today—and a small section of another—I clocked in at 1,440 words, before editing, and I liked most of them. Piss off, reaper.)

5

WHO

I thought it was a joke at first. I almost chuckled in a good-natured way. Then I realized she wasn't kidding, and I stifled the laugh. She'd just said, "*My book doesn't really fall into a genre because it fits all fiction categories and would be fun for people who like all genres.*"

Listen, there could very well be a person out there who reads every genre. This person may also like every kind of music. (I can't tell you how many times I've heard that nonsense. Oh, really? So if I put opera, ragtime, and hillbilly folk on shuffle you'll be happy as a clam?)

Good luck finding this unicorn.

It sounds so evolved to say you love all music and every genre, but the average consumer of books—we're talking the ones who will put down money in enough numbers to make your writing career sustainable—are notoriously dedicated to one or two types of stories.

They may like romance and mysteries, but never touch horror. They bury themselves in fantasy novels and wouldn't dream of picking up a memoir. Or they can't get enough thrillers in their queue, yet ignore supernatural graphic novels.

To which I say: *So what?* It's not like you get cool points for reading eleven different genres a month. We like what we like.

Some people can't abide your taste in books; it irritates them, and that puzzles the shit out of me. They find out you've never read a single real-crime book and they hound you to try it. But you don't want to. And why do they care?

This falls into the same category of people worrying themselves to death over your taste in food. "*You don't like sushi? Oh, you have to try it again. Come with me, and I'll take you to the best spot.*"

No. I don't like it. I don't mind that *you* like it. Jesus, leave me alone.

People have specific tastes, and the sooner you accept the fact that they just might not care for your collection of country-singer-vampire novels is not a personal indictment of your capabilities as a writer.

(Although, suddenly, I think I'd like to pen a story about a country singer who's a vampire. That combination just popped into my head as a joke, but I think I like it. Has anyone done that yet?)

Your book, no matter how great it is, will have an audience, and only that particular audience. Nobody has ever written a book that everyone can agree on. *Go, Dog. Go!* may be the closest we'll ever come, because it's pretty freakin' spectacular. That party up in the tree at the end? C'mon.

(During the edit stage of this book I just had to check,

and it turns out that six percent of people on Amazon gave it one star. See what I mean about pleasing everyone? Who gives *Go, Dog. Go!* one star? Some people are just assholes.)

But let's look at this from your point of view as a writer. We've already talked about overcoming fear, and we've touched on battling insecurity. Your mindset about the potential audience for your words can play a huge role in overcoming both debilitating emotions.

Unless you've truly tapped into some sort of cosmic creative zone that defies categorization—and sorry, but you haven't—your posse of readers are zealous about what they like. The goal is to get them to like *you*. Forget about everyone else. I'm sure they're nice people. Have coffee with them, trade recipes, go to a ballgame together. But stop trying to coerce them into buying your words.

THEN COMES A PRETTY important step in your evolution as a writer. Since we've determined there's one ideal reader for your work, have you taken the time to figure out who they are? Because once you do, you'll stand a better chance of delivering what they want, along with deliveries to the thousands (or millions) of clones who share their literary-taste DNA.

Here's the way I did this.

Of the many genres I've dabbled in, middle-grade fiction has been one of the more challenging. To start with, it's competitive as hell, with a gaggle of new authors popping up every week. For some strange reason, many people interested in writing believe it's somehow easier to do this genre because they think the readers aren't advanced. The theory, I guess, is that a fourth- or fifth-grader won't be too demanding, nor will they be picky.

Bullshit. They're pretty goddamned demanding and picky.

And their tastes are almost as varied as a grown-up's. They know what they like, even if it's only because their peers like it. Kids wanna be part of a tribe. It's how they navigate the social minefields of late-elementary school and middle school.

(Side note: If you're writing for middle-school students, just know that peer review often plays a big role in your success. It's a shitty time for most kids—it was for me—and they wanna be liked. If a popular group likes Author X, everyone around them will glom on.)

I tried out a specific type of book for middle-graders. Writing under the pen name Buster Blank, I crafted a freaky, bizarro story that incorporated humor and a touch of gross-out.

Now, not every kid will like that, just like the adults we referenced a few paragraphs ago. But many do. And by donating several dozen copies to schools I was able to get feedback. I visited classrooms and did presentations after they'd read the weird book. I solicited their opinions, which they freely gave. And something clicked.

I found that my target for Buster Blank tales was a kid in fourth or fifth grade who liked quirky stories. No stories about girls and horses (although those can be very popular). No coming-of-age saga. No *Hunger Games* or *Percy Jackson* clones.

The books I crafted for these students felt like *The*

Twilight Zone for nine-year-olds. The kids who dug that stuff would eat up any additional volumes matching that tag. And they did. Buster now has (as of this writing) three books in the marketplace, with a fourth due soon, and others forthcoming.

HERE'S something for you to consider as you start down the writing road. Defining *who* is going to read your work is as important as figuring out *what* to write.

Who is she/he?

Who is catering to them now?

And what is it about detective books that turns them on? Or romance. Or sci-fi. Or whatever. There's some niche in a genre that either is being underserved for them or could stand a fresh voice.

Who? Because just sitting down to write and saying "*Everyone will love this*" is a sure way to flop.

Maybe take a day, or even just a few hours in one day, to chew on this project.

ONE LAST THING TO make this less like a homework assignment and more like an inspiring caress. Defining who will plop down $3 or $5 or $25 for your words actually makes it much easier to compose those words.

In the radio business we're often coached to visualize the average listener in our target demographic. There were times when managers and consultants would even name this person. *"Dom, you're speaking to a woman named*

Claire. She's thirty-eight, a mom, and works full-time while raising her kids."

It sounds cheesy as shit, and in some ways it is. But, at the core, it *does* work. Imagining the person who would enjoy our show allows us to structure the content for it. Sure, lots of other people besides Claire tune in, and many of them don't share a damned thing in common with her. But there's spillover in every business endeavor. Finding the core listener for a radio show is a good place to start.

Finding your core reader is just as critical. Quit trying to please everyone, and start pleasing Claire. Or Sarah. Or Sarah's weird brother, Tony. It will make your job easier, and even more enjoyable. You'll feel like you're not only creating something, you're *serving* someone.

And serving sells.

6

NOTES

The title and description of this chapter were jotted down in a notebook. A blue, seventy-page, college-ruled, school notebook. I think I got it on sale a couple of Augusts ago for fifty cents.

I love notebooks. It's practically a compulsion, and if I'm buying one I'm likely buying three. Office supplies are my crack, just way cheaper and without any need of intervention. I mean, they even have an intoxicating smell. You may or may not relate with that.

You should work in whatever format you like, and whatever format is most conducive to creating good words. Personally, I straddle the digital and analog worlds. My laptop gets the bulk of play, but those paper notebooks are indispensable. When I'm sitting at a bar or restaurant, they're my go-to because they're easily transported and require no plug.

(Side note: Just last night I sat at a bar, alone, during happy hour, and this time I did have my laptop. Sure enough, another person had to make some derogatory comment, "*What kind of loser works at a bar?*" I always laugh at these dumbasses. Don't they know it's not *work*? We love to write, and we can do it any goddamned place we feel like it. I'm not there to win the Cool Guy of The Year award. I'm there to drink my whiskey and Coke and crank out a chapter. So piss off.)

Plenty of writers use digital note-taking apps, and my cell phone is chock-full of dictated ideas. But there's something about ink on paper that I connect with. You may be the same way.

They're terrific tools for fleshing out thin, newborn ideas. Even halfway through writing a piece of fiction I'll break out a notebook and plot a course for the next few chapters. This has come in handy more than once when a story has been left unattended for weeks or months.

History describes many notable folks as notetakers. Thomas Jefferson reportedly kept seven notebooks going at a time, recording everything from the growth and migration of wildlife and fauna to his political observations.

Mark Twain tried out sentence structure for some of his most popular witticisms. There are pages of his notebooks showing the evolution of these lines, with early versions scribbled then marked through. Eventually satisfied, the finished product would make its way into one of his books.

And according to legend, filmmaker George Lucas hurriedly pulled out a notebook when, during post-production on his film *American Graffiti*, a sound editor asked for Reel 2, Dialogue 2. Or, as he said it in film jargon, R2D2. To George, it just sounded cool and might be something he could use in another film.

Landmark moments like this could easily come and then flit away without our trusty notebooks.

I'm writing this chapter as a warning, though, if you share my notebook fetish. *Don't let them become graveyards*. In other words, they can't become the places where ideas go to die.

It's happened to me plenty, maybe because at any given time I have two or three notebooks going at once. (Thomas Jefferson would call me a slacker.) Things get logged, then hastily forgotten when the page is turned. I start every entry with the date, which might not be the best idea. It's too easy to flip backward and curse the visual proof that you've dallied for ages on a particular "great" idea.

And—this may sound weird—sometimes I wonder if old, handwritten notes don't engender the same respect as their digital counterparts. For whatever reason, as much as I love the venerable, old notebook, I don't seem to take its contents as seriously as something banged out on Scrivener or another electronic workhorse.

But, in some nebulous way, I have to have them. As much of a mess as mine are, with little-to-no order whatsoever, the notebooks act as a security blanket. Their contents are comforting, because they represent ideas and outlines in their purest, rawest forms. What you scribble with a pen is ultimately much less refined than anything you keep in a laptop. Your pen has no backspace key.

But let's get back to the earlier warning, the one in

italics that mentioned graveyards. And let me employ a roundabout analogy.

For years it was assumed that the best way to ensure you followed through with a resolution was to share it with other people. For instance, if you wanted to become a published author, you were supposed to announce it to the world. "*Hey, everyone, I'm gonna write a book!*"

The thinking was that, by speaking it aloud, it applied the pressure you needed to reach your goal. Nobody wants to embarrass themselves by failing on a stated goal, right? If you told people you were gonna do it, you damned well better do it.

We've all heard this. It sounds reasonable, and so we go around spouting off all our goals.

And it turns out it's bullshit.

Recent studies have determined that you're actually *less* likely to follow through if you tell other people. Yes, if you tell your circle of friends you're gonna write a book in the next year, you're creating a jinx. It's better, they say, to keep it to yourself.

Upon examination, the reason makes sense. Speaking the words, it seems, creates what's known as an identity goal. In a piece in 2009 in *Psychological Science*, researchers pointed out that the simple act of stating your goal—in our specific case, "*I'm gonna write a book!*"—causes your mind to interpret that as already accomplishing part of that goal. In other words, you're halfway there.

And when you're halfway there, your drive is reduced.

Nobody argues that having a goal isn't important. It definitely is. But it's possible that the goal is more likely to be achieved when we keep it to ourselves. In other words, shut up and write.

Whew, that was a long way to get to the point. Sorry.

The point is that your notebooks, or wherever you keep your ideas and outlines, have the potential of creating a similar identity goal. If you've written three pages of notes for an article, your brain may feel like you've accomplished the task or at least pored over it to the extent that it's practically written.

I find this interesting, and it definitely resonates. For the longest time I kept individual notebooks for various projects. One for a young adult mystery series I was writing (there was even a different notebook for each volume in the series), one for some middle-grade books, and another for a nonfiction piece. Each was a collection of ideas and planning, with potential plots for the fiction and potential chapters and marketing efforts for the nonfiction.

And I went back to them over and over again. During times where I should've been writing the damned books, I was scratching more shit into those notebooks. In some ways, it became easier to keep planning than to implement the freaking plans.

So the million-dollar question is: *Where do you draw the line*? We want to get our thoughts down before they vanish—we want to be prepared to write—but we don't want to screw with our mind.

Don't eliminate your notes entirely. They provide strong foundations for the words yet to come. Organization is good. You may simply need to cut back on your notes. This book, for instance, barely has any notes associated with it. Most of my ideas were digital, and they occupied a total of two pages in a document. No separate notebook devoted entirely to *The Color of Your Dreams*.

Less planning, more writing, which was totally by design. And, whatta ya know? The manuscript rounded into form much more quickly than the young adult mystery with its multiple notebooks. Coincidence?

Your notebooks are good because they're a security blanket. They're bad for the same reason. How *much* you rely on them for security is what matters here. Are they supplying you with warm encouragement, or are they an overprotective parent?

7
———

COPYCATS

One of the joys of working with a major publisher in New York has been the opportunity to speak at various conferences and seminars around the country. You not only meet scores of great readers, but you also mingle and interact with other writers, including those in your genre(s). You share stories from your writing path, and you learn that you're not the only weirdo in the world after all.

Writers are generally weird. You almost have to be.

Anyway.

At a conference a few years ago I sat on a panel with four other writers of young adult fiction, the room packed with school librarians. It was a fun session, with lots of information exchanged and plenty of laughs, too. The questions from the librarians were thoughtful, and I think everyone in the room—both the audience *and* the panel members—left with new insights into young adult readers.

Afterward, I spoke with one of the other writers on

the panel. He was charming and witty, giddy about his soon-to-be-released book—his first—and deservedly proud of his three-book contract. We chatted about the conference, our writing processes, and our various influences. It was a great talk.

And then he said something interesting. He told me he was a huge fan of a certain author who'd struck gold in the past three years. I mean, a *major* vein of YA riches. He was such a fan of this author, in fact, that he said he'd written a story exactly like the ones in this hit series.

His words: "*Exactly like them.*"

I blinked at him a few times. Then I asked for clarification: "*You mean you wrote a book exactly like that? Plot, characters, everything?*"

"*Yep,*" he said. And an agent had loved it and a publisher had signed him.

Then we talked about the disappointing dessert at lunch.

I actually was able to digest the lunch much better than the story of his publishing journey. Listen, I would never tell you how to go about your writing and would certainly never poo-poo someone's three-book contract. Those don't just fall off trees, you know.

But to show pride at copying another writer's story— merely changing the setting and the characters' names— to land a deal?

People are different. I'd never be able to do it. And I'm a bit disgusted at both the agent and the publisher for validating it.

It's funny, because I've told people about ideas I've had for stories, and occasionally I'll hear, "*Yeah, I read a book with that same storyline.*" And I curse for about an hour, research their claim, and, if the book does exist, throw my notes in the trash and move on. This just happened again within the past month, actually. And it was such a *great* idea. Dammit!

Someone once told me my *Galahad* series of books for young adults was similar to another book they'd read. I was anxious and more than a little pissed, until I discovered this other book had come out four years after the first *Galahad* book. Whew.

It's said there are no new ideas. It's also said that every work of fiction follows the same basic premise, e.g., the hero's journey. And, additionally, we know that subconscious pilfering happens. C'mon, there are more than a million books published every year. Crossover will happen. Songwriters deal with this all the time. Have you seen all the lawsuits filed over similar melodies?

So I get that. But *intentionally* chasing a hit by mirroring another?

The desire for fame and fortune is intense. Gobs of surveys have pointed out that the primary aspiration of Americans under the age of twenty-five is not a great job, nor a beautiful home, nor even a fulfilling relationship. It's to be famous.

I'm not criticizing that. People can want whatever they want, and why would I care? At the same time, though, it does play a role, in my opinion, in the relaxing of the ethical standards involving plagiarism. When your driving force isn't pride but rather fame, then integrity be damned.

"Yeah, I just wrote a book about an orphaned boy who's a wizard and goes off to wizarding school. You'll love it!"

Maybe it doesn't even register with some people that this is at all questionable. It irks the crap out of *me*, but they see no problem. I'm not sure if that's a generational thing or what. Probably not. It's likely just the times we occupy.

Scanning the bestseller lists, I get the feeling that a sizable portion of the writing/reading universe has no beef with different authors replicating successful books. In fact, many readers may *crave* copycats, regardless of who pens them.

And that's a strong possibility. Hollywood moguls lose no sleep whatsoever over this issue. As soon as a movie about a bird who's a private eye with a cat partner makes $100 million at the box office, within ten months you'll see a badger private eye movie and hear about the lemur PI that's in pre-production.

(By the way, I just pulled the bird/cat crime-fighting idea straight out of my ass, so it's available if you're interested in writing a script. I don't think it's been done. Yet. Better hurry.)

After speaking at schools for years, I'll vouch for the fact that many young readers are so enraptured by a particular book series that they read every volume over and over again. They won't touch anything else because they simply can't get enough of that one series and its characters. Which is fantastic news for the authors who create *those* books.

All of this adds to the hypnotic appeal of copycatting. Success breeds imitation (and lust for that same success) and sometimes the target audience won't (for a time) accept anything else. So the temptation is damned strong.

I'm encouraging you to seek another path. Shortcuts to fame and riches are there for the taking, and if that's all that motivates you, so be it. But I hope there are other, more soul-enriching motives beating within your chest.

Speaking of which . . .

8

ENGINE

I f you haven't read Hugh Howey's blog posts and articles, you should. You'll appreciate Hugh's candor about the publishing industry, especially his critical observations of traditional publishing versus the indie route.

On top of that, the guy has sold a veritable shitload of books. Just not at first. And *that's* a great starting point for a discussion about what's driving you as a writer. Identifying what powers your engine may not necessarily make you a better writer, but I believe it'll provide a little more clarity to the journey.

Let's get back to Hugh. This guy put out roughly half a dozen books before ever sniffing anything resembling a hit. And that doesn't count the pieces he wrote without publishing.

Now, put yourself in his place and answer truthfully: After "failing" once, twice, three times, would you keep it up? After the fourth book failed to attract attention, would you publish the fifth? Then a sixth?

Would you muster the resolve to write that seventh book?

Sure, on the surface you say, "*Hell yeah!*" But that reflection on the surface hides a lot of pain in the depths, man. A *lot* of pain. Writing, editing, and publishing a novel takes vast supplies of inner strength. It takes patience and the right attitude.

And it takes humility. In fact, that may be the most critical ingredient. When your family and friends know you're pumping out title after title, and they know how badly you want to see your name on the shelves at the bookstore—but they know, too, that it ain't happening . . .

Well, it does something to you. I rarely hear authors talk about this, but when people ask you, "*So, you workin' on a new book?*" and they ask it with that shitty smirk on their face, you better damned well be strong. It's easy to crumble under the embarrassment. Your friends don't know that more than a million other authors are competing with you that year. All they know is that you put out a book and it wasn't made into a movie.

Which, as dumb as it may sound, is the yardstick by which many people judge every title. "*When's it gonna be a movie?*"

And you want to change the subject. Or scream. Or punch them in the neck. "*I'm a writer, dammit. Does every-thing have to be a fucking movie?*"

This is the element of being an author that's generally not talked about: the pressure we put on ourselves to live up to silly ideals created by others. We get trapped into thinking that if you're gonna be a writer, you're gonna see the words *New York Times Bestseller* embossed on the paperback's cover.

And yet the math tells us that more than 999,500 of those million authors won't have a hit, won't have a movie, and won't get to rub their fingers over any happy-ass embossing on the cover.

Here's an example. I did well with my first book—in my hometown. The book won some pretty cool awards, even an international grand prize, but the bulk of the actual sales was centered within one hundred miles of my house. I was a Colorado hit with that first title, but not a national one, despite the international award.

After almost three hundred people queued up at a bookstore in Denver to hear me speak and to get signed copies—giving me a huge rush—I boarded a plane for Houston. I spoke at a conference, and afterward my publisher set me up with a signing at a small, indepen-dent book store near Rice University. No marketing, no advertising, no nothing. There wasn't a sign in the store to say I'd be there. I think even the manager was surprised to see me. He quickly set up some folding chairs.

One of my old high school buddies had moved to Houston, so I invited him and he showed up out of curiosity.

Along with one other person, who just happened to be in the store. One. And that guy didn't buy a copy of the book. He just listened to my brief talk, asked a couple of questions, then wandered off.

My friend had to be thinking, "*Dom is a complete failure as an author.*" I wanted to tell him, "*Dude, I just crushed it with three hundred people in Colorado!*" But his eyeballs told him *one person*, so I didn't say anything.

A friend of mine, John Shors, has written several terrific books, and today he's very successful. But after his first book's release, when he was essentially an unknown author, he did a reading and book signing in a park—coincidentally also in Houston—where literally no one was there when he started. A few dozen folding chairs sat empty while he stood up under a canopy of tall trees and just started reading aloud to no one.

After a while he had to laugh. Which caught someone's attention as they ambled past in the park. Which caused them to stop and listen to this lunatic standing there, alone, narrating a book with tears of laughter spilling down his cheeks.

Which caused other people to stop and see what the spectacle was. And then a few more. Soon the seats filled up.

John tells the story way better than I do. But he's a bestselling author who, at the start of his career, read his book to empty seats in a park.

If you're not humble and thick-skinned, do not take on this journey. But if you can smile through the pain and persevere with a good attitude, you can rise above.

Unless you're in Houston, apparently. Then you're screwed.

OUR FRIENDS, our families, and total strangers equate publishing with instant success. Just the words "*published author*" convey an image to most people that you're the shit. If they see you at a book signing with one or two lonely souls in the vast array of folding chairs, they tilt their head like a dog staring at a fan.

John Shors dealt with it. Hugh Howey put up with that nonsense seven times. They both kept writing. J.K. Rowling famously was rejected more than a dozen times —and told to "get a day job"—before Harry Potter busted wide open.

Joann Harris wrote a novel that eventually became a Johnny Depp film, but *Chocolat* was turned down so many times that Harris said she "made a sculpture" out of the rejection slips.

THIS IS where we find out what's driving you. What kind of engine is under your hood? And this isn't a trick question. Something is ultimately behind your drive to write, but there's perhaps something even more personal that drives you to publish.

I'll go first.

When I was in elementary school and middle school, my dad was in the military. We moved every couple of years, so I was always the new kid. If you've been a new kid, you know it's a challenge.

Wait, that's the politically-correct way to say it. If you've been the new kid, you know it usually fucking sucks. Kids have their cliques firmly in place, and they got no time for some jerk who just arrived from Michigan or Alaska or wherever. To say the least, I wasn't welcomed with open arms, nor treated very well.

But out of pain comes inspiration. I turned to books,

getting lost in adventures that didn't involve seventh-grade shitheads. My literary heroes were Jules Verne, Arthur C. Clarke, Michael Crichton, and Franklin W. Dixon. They never laughed at me in the hallways or ignored me at recess.

Their tales did something more than just keep me company, though. They triggered something inside me you might understand. Gradually, I began to believe I could tell a story, too. I had zero interest whatsoever in letting another person read them. I wrote for me, and you could say my engine was powered by a need to escape.

But we evolve. Today I have a happy life. Sure, there are still a few lingering shitheads, but my engine now is powered by a desire to stretch my skills, exploring different styles. I've published in five different genres, and each time I work my ass off to make that particular book better than the last one.

It's like the height lines that parents pencil onto a door, showing the growth of their children through the years. I measure each work by the line before it. And I damned well better be growing.

So that's what drives me.

WHY DO *YOU* WRITE?

YOUR FIRST ANSWER will be wrong. And whatever answer you eventually settle upon stands a good chance of being different five years from now.

Why is the answer often elusive? If you ask people

why they're cops or nurses or teachers, they'll likely tell you without hesitation. And five years from now they'll likely give the same answer.

But writing, although it *can* be a profession, is more apt to fall under the mystical category of a calling. I think the reasons we write are difficult to pin down because we're not even completely sure what the hell it is we're doing. Seems to depend on the day. Or the hour of the day.

And your journey can splinter off into an almost-limitless number of trails, each inspired by a unique desire.

Andrea might be moved to write a memoir about raising a child with autism. On the surface you could deduce that she wants to help other families facing the same challenge, and I'm sure that plays a part. But if you sat down with Andrea, shared a few glasses of wine and talked late into the night about the real *Why*, there's a good chance you'd find she honestly needs to funnel her emotions into written form. It would be her personal therapy.

Brooke worked in corporate America for fifteen years before burning out and walking away. Within two years she'd opened a yoga studio and spent six days a week helping people—many of them people working in the same high-stress world Brooke had escaped—to center themselves. By writing a how-to business book, outlining the strategies for transitioning from one career to another, her *Why* comes from a place of celebration. "*I did it, and you can, too!*"

Marc grew up reading science fiction and fantasy

books, was the picked-on kid in school, felt unappreciated and misunderstood, and discovered that writing opened a door to a new life while closing the door on his painful past. His stories provide an escape for people hiding the same scars.

Perhaps what Andrea, Brooke, and Marc sought was a connection. These come in a variety of flavors, but each powerful in their own way. Through writing, Andrea and Marc may have succeeded in forging an *internal* connection, today often referred to as mindfulness. Brooke may have longed for a connection with *others*. Both forms, the connection with self and with others, touch the boundaries of the spiritual. Both provide substantial motivation.

WHY DO *YOU* WRITE? You might have dreams of bestseller status when you first start pecking out words on a screen. That's why we're always wrong when we first think about the *Why*. Yeah, we want our words to be read, and we want our books/articles/posts/whatever to be accepted.

But things like bestseller charts, royalties, and Hollywood don't represent the real *Why*. There's always something submerged, something that keeps us coming back to the keyboard. Something urging us to write these particular words, something that eventually frees us to express the unconscious desires of the id.

Relax, I'm not going to get deep into Freudian shit with you. But take a breath and slog through this with me for one minute, because I'm fascinated by the Austrian neurologist's musings on the human mind. And if, for the sake of argument, we accept Sigmund's structural model of the psyche, it may actually bring you peace in your creative desires.

If the id is indeed the dark, unconscious chaos that Freud supposed, embrace the living shit out of it. Because it represents instinct without organization. Moreover, the id wants two things: satisfaction and pleasure.

Well, the *Why* of your writing pursuit will ideally emanate from the same place. Not to sell books. Not to attract thousands of drooling fans to a book signing. It should provide satisfaction and pleasure to your soul.

Yes, we want the good things in life. But you're a writer. Your words need to, on that unconscious level, bring you pleasure long before you see tangible rewards. They should sate the invisible beast and then proudly represent your inner drive.

Your dreams may be blue or red or green, but those colors have shades, and you won't really see those shades until you hold up the prism of your life. Until you find the experience, or the emotion, that drives you.

AND NOW, in the spirit of full disclosure, I'll fess up. As important as it is, *just getting better* is actually the second-biggest driving factor in my writing life. My ultimate motivation is far from noble.

I basically write in order to give the middle finger to all of those assholes I encountered in middle school.

Whatever gets it done, right?

Why do *you* write?

9

SHORTIES

My first attempt at a novel was a grandiose piece called *Those Who Help Themselves*. I had what I believed to be a very mature, thought-provoking title, a rough concept of a main character, and absolutely no real storyline or plot whatsoever.

I was twelve years old.

When that effort went down in flames after a day or two of heavy thoughts, I went back to scribbling out short bursts of fan fiction—a couple of *Star Trek* stories, as I recall, dreaming up new adventures for Kirk, Spock, and McCoy. Those were fun. Probably dreadful, but damned fun.

Then came another inspired idea for a novel, a science fiction adventure, which didn't survive until dinner that night. I don't even remember the title of that one, but I know it involved a Council. All science fiction novels, I think, must have a Council. It's a law or something.

(When, years later, I wrote my young adult *Galahad*

series, I made sure to include the required Council, so I wouldn't be embarrassed at conventions when someone yelled, "*Hey, where's the freakin' Council, ya loser?*")

Novels are damned hard to write. Yet, for some reason, many people equate *all* writing with novel writing. You may have told someone you write short stories and received the same look people exhibit when they get their first-ever glimpse under the hood of a car.

Short fiction used to be looked upon with great favor. It was a revered form of storytelling, and celebrated novelists (as mentioned in the previous chapter) enjoyed tossing out 5,000-word mini-dramas as much as, if not more than, their famous, sometimes-bloated masterpieces.

Then, a few decades ago, the short story lost its luster with the mainstream, and the only thing anyone wanted to talk about was the latest bestselling novel. Writers eschewed anything with fewer than 80,000 words. Beginning writers were faced with the daunting task of selling novels and nothing but.

Sure, there have been some great short stories written in the last few years. Novelists like Stephen King and John Grisham, a couple of 800-pound gorillas on the sales charts, have published pretty badass short fiction. (If you haven't read King's collection called *Night Shift* or Grisham's *Ford County*, put a bookmark here and go devour them now. I'll wait.) Alice Munro has received not only acclaim and huge sales numbers for her short work, but a Nobel Prize.

The emphasis these days, however, clearly falls on the full-length book because that's what gets attention. So you'd think I'd encourage you to crank out a big, fat novel. Nope. My advice is to shelve the big book you dream about and get busy on shorties.

Four reasons.

ONE: You need the practice.

Look, no pouting. I'm sure your prose is delicious, and your family and friends have raved. Cool.

But *everyone* needs the practice. A well-crafted short story forces you to create a swift-moving, cohesive, well-planned story. You learn how to cut the crap, to eliminate needless filler that *we* fall in love with but that mostly irritates the piss out of our readers.

You get a better sense of the winning structure in all good storytelling: beginning (introduce characters, put their asses in trouble), middle (create tension, unveil new conflict, build to the climax), and end (uh, the end). And you do all of this quickly, in only a few thousand words instead of some J.K. Rowling-sized anvil.

(That's no knock on Ms. Rowling, I'm just being sarcastic. I truly love her anvils.)

TWO: It builds confidence.

And you *need* confidence. I don't think I'm wrong in supposing that 95 percent of people reading this book have started at least one novel and never finished it. You know what that does? It makes you feel like a failure, and you're not a failure. Remember what I said several paragraphs ago: Novels are damned hard to write.

At every stage of your writing career you should bang out a short story or ten, but especially at the beginning of your journey. Finish a killer short story, publish it (even if just online), and you feel like a million bucks, whether it sells or not. You did it. You started a great story, and you *finished* it. You saw it through to publication. You are published. That shit goes on your writing resume, and editors and agents might appreciate it.

I'd recommend doing it again before you take on a novel. In fact, get a pretty good collection of short stories under your belt. You'll have a terrific grasp of story structure and you'll be strutting.

THREE: It establishes you.

Yes, we all want to come out of the gate with a million-selling novel, one of those great Cinderella stories of publishing. People praise you as a sparkling new talent, and you're an instant source of inspiration for millions of people who yearn for success.

That's a sweet story, but what's with this shortcut-mania our culture has bought into? Shows like *American Idol*, with its fawning worship of overnight sensations who never paid their damned dues, are endemic of the scourge. Yeah, some had remarkable success. Most didn't. Meanwhile, the vast majority of great artists built their reputation through years of plying their trade, practicing, playing countless shows, evolving. *Learning.*

Pay the dues. Do the time. Write the stories. Build your following. Establish yourself as a writer to be trusted. Overnight sensations make for great copy in places like *People* magazine, but real artisans don't spring up. They develop.

Writing dozens or hundreds of articles, essays, blog posts, and short fiction will establish you in the minds of readers and, again, people in the publishing business. When you *do* publish a novel, your writer's cred will pay dividends.

FOUR: It's much more fun.

Okay, maybe not for everyone. But I speak for a lot of writers who know that knocking out a killer short story— or essay, or feature article—is a hoot. Writing a novel, quite honestly, can be downright tedious. It's months (or years) of work, hitting dead ends, forgetting what you wrote about a particular character five months ago, or flat-out losing interest.

Yes, finishing a novel is rapturous. Writing it? Not so much.

I think that's why getting an idea for a short story is so thrilling. It's something you can do in a week or two, maybe even a day or two. And that rush we get at the start of a writing project doesn't have time to fade into the shadow of drudgery like a novel might do.

You stay in the blush of new love.

WHEN I WAS ABOUT thirty years old I was newly-divorced and, to be frank, mired in some pretty bad depression. My professional world was fine, working at a top-rated radio station. My personal life, however, was not so rosy.

It was during this next year that I rediscovered writing, something I'd enjoyed as an adolescent but had ignored for many years. My gloomy frame of mind during that point in my life is remarkably evident in the short stories that I began to write.

Dark? They were positively creepy. It was catharsis in perhaps its purest form, the purging of emotional tension. When I finished one, I began another. They came in a gush, at least half a dozen in just a couple of months.

I think if I'd tried to crank out a novel at this point in my life I would've failed miserably. I wasn't ready to invest the time and emotional equity into a *project*. I needed to stay busy and to move from piece to piece.

Today I still credit that dark period of my life with jump-starting my writing career. Would I have been successful as a writer if my personal life hadn't imploded briefly? I don't know. Maybe.

What I do know is that my creative energy was focused into short bursts, like running sprints. That undoubtedly built up my stamina, and it injected confidence. It happened at just the right time.

(A few of those stories, by the way, showed up years later in a collection of short fiction I published. *Wednesday, and Other Dark Tales* was released under one of my various pen names.)

YOU WANT WINS, especially early on. You don't have to win the championship on your first go, just snag quick, minor victories that give you experience, teach you, build up your confidence, establish your bonafides, and keep a smile on your face.

There are plenty of outlets hungry for short fiction and many even embrace new, previously-unpublished writers. Scan the most recent edition of *Writer's Market* for some of these publications or the back pages of *Writer's Digest*. Look for submission calls from anthologies. Scour library shelves for contemporary literary magazines and note their submission requirements. Opportunities won't come looking for you; it's the other way around.

Start small. The big payoff is coming.

10

RECONSIDERATION

My mom passed away when I was still a young man, only twenty-one. And that sucks. We take our parents for granted—you know we do—and just about the time I reached the age where I finally appreciated my mother's wit and wisdom she was stolen from me.

On more than one occasion she used the word "*reconsider*" while shepherding me through adolescence. There was a time, when I was seventeen, where I was boiling about something at work, some grievance I had with the boss. I was a young radio disc jockey, full of piss and vinegar, thinking (naturally) that I already knew it all, and I fumed over a perceived lack of respect. The particular incident itself isn't even relevant.

I stormed about the house like a petulant child. I vented to my mother about how unfair it was. I got worked up enough to tell her that I was going to call the station's program director and threaten to walk out the door for good. That would show him.

"Think you might want to reconsider that?" she asked. And the way she did it was classic: not looking at me, supposedly busy with some other trivial duty, just going about her business and idly wondering aloud. Her tone of voice wasn't aggressive or judgmental, just curious, really.

But that question. "*Think you might want to reconsider that?*"

And, of course, I did reconsider. I cooled off, got my shit together, and went to work. Years later I can't help but wonder if I'd even have this long career in radio if I'd acted on my irrational, teenage impulses. Probably not.

THIS IS WHERE YOU, after patiently wading through almost three hundred words of an anecdote, say: "*What's the point of this goddamned story?*"

Reconsideration is one of the best actions a writer can take. Most people use a different word for it. They call it editing.

I call it reconsideration.

WE START by falling in love with an idea. Then we begin a torrid affair with characters, ushering them to life from some mystical place we'll never quite understand. We populate our stories with people and places and conflict and a climax, and we call it good.

Then we must hand our baby over to an editor.

And we fear the editor. It's the person who can do the most good to our story, and we fear him or her.

It has nothing to do with the person. Editors are often good people, often writers themselves, professionals who have mastered the art of cutting through our bullshit and seeing the guts of a story. It's not their skills that we fear or abhor; it's the fear of our own shortcomings.

A quality editor quickly sees where we fail and saves us. She points out the follies within our plots and the excessive word vomit within our dialogue. She strives to take our great idea, that original block of marble, and cut away everything that doesn't ultimately produce Michelangelo's David.

For this she is simultaneously appreciated and resented. Yes, we want her to make the work better, but in some respects we may see her as the concentrated embodiment of the faceless public touched on earlier, the public whose judgment we quietly fear. She sees our writing in its original form, words suffering from bedhead and morning breath.

So it's a *grudging* alliance. Why? Because we are artists. We're supposed to be able to do this ourselves.

Ah, but the writing genius and the editing genius rarely occupy the same real estate. Are you a good writer? Do you want to be a better writer?

Then get over yourself, quickly. Find an honest editor.

THE FIRST PROFESSIONAL editor with whom I worked was a woman named Dorsey. She lived in the mountains of Colorado, and she came highly recommended. I was new to the tough, sometimes cruel world of publishing and book sales but knew enough to seek out real help to make my YA novel the best it could be.

I wasn't prepared for my first conversation with Dorsey after she'd plowed through the flawed draft I sent her. The problem was that I didn't *know* it was flawed. I thought it was good.

Dorsey asked a lot of questions after reading that manuscript:

"Did you mean to (fill in the blank)?"

"Why would this character (fill in the blank)?"

"Don't you think they would (fill in the blank)?"

In other words, she didn't tell me to do a goddamned thing. She asked questions. She made me . . .

She made me *reconsider* my novel.

Yes, it was a good story. The idea for it was good from the get-go. I'd imagined interesting characters and an adventurous plot that spoke to the ten-year-old me—for that was my target market.

But, in the myopic rush of writing, I'd galloped past details that would expand the depth of the story, would add a layer beneath the surface scenes, and generally make it a better book.

My editor did more than clean up the story. She truly helped me to reconsider what the story *could be*.

Because, when you get right down to it, that's what we need the most: Someone with a critical but fair eye. Someone who doesn't tell us how to write the book, but rather helps us to understand *why* we write the book. (Which is the focus of the next chapter, by the way.)

From the beginning I told Dorsey of my love of adventure books as a young boy. I told her how libraries became almost a place of worship for a kid who moved as often as I did. I wanted to capture that love of adventure and repurpose it for a new audience of word-hungry kids.

I had the basic story. But I'd never considered—truly considered—what those characters could be, how they could speak to my young self and to the millions of young readers I wanted to reach.

She gently worked with me so that I could reconsider the book through the eyes of its intended readers. Her questions were just what I needed. She listened to my answers and either nodded or asked a follow-up.

And—this is key—I trusted her. If you sincerely want to make your book the best it can be, if you can swallow your creative pride, and if you're open to fresh perspectives on your work, then trust. Trust that they know what ingredients are missing from the cake.

A FEW YEARS LATER, after being signed to a multi-book contract by Tor/Macmillan, a new editor entered my world. Susan's role was a bit different from Dorsey's. She not only was responsible for ensuring the quality of each individual book, she became a counselor of sorts for the series as a whole.

That's not as simple a job as you might think. Maintaining the integrity of a six-book series through each volume requires attention to not only details of the moment, but an almost seer-like ability to envision the entire arc. In short, her job included keeping me focused on the endgame.

We didn't always see eye to eye, and she likely grew

frustrated with me on more than one occasion. Listen, the relationship between writer and editor isn't supposed to be a love affair. If you and your editor agree one hundred percent of the time, it's time for you to find a new editor.

The relationship is similar to a business arrangement, but one that exists outside the world of exact, definitive answers. You're not dealing with a spreadsheet or blueprint. You're dealing with art, and you're two passionate individuals collaborating to create something ethereal.

The best editors are imminently qualified to help shape your vision. Sometimes you'll alter it, sometimes you won't. Just be sure that your ego is in check, or there's no point in hiring an editor in the first place.

Ultimately, I've been supremely blessed. Both Dorsey Moore and Susan Chang helped to craft the *Galahad* series into something that will always make me proud. And, even more important, both women made me a better writer. I owe them momentous gratitude. Should you ever have the chance to work with either, consider yourself one lucky writer.

ARE you prepared to reconsider your story? You've breathed life into the embryonic idea, and you've (hopefully) fleshed it out. It has the basic structure and details.

But have you really considered what your story is supposed to *do* to your reader? I hadn't. I thought I had, but I really hadn't.

A good editor will help you with that. Find them. Then listen to them.

11

PROCESS

Of all the skills that can help you successfully publish your words, perhaps the one that draws the least attention is the discipline of establishing a process. I understand why it lurks in the shadows, because writing is supposed to be exotic, almost sexy, and developing a process is so *unsexy*.

But too bad. You can read books on writing, you can jot down pages and pages of ideas, and you can spend hours building a website that makes you appear to be a real writer. But if you don't have a process in place to actually transform the idea into a published piece, you might stall before getting too far.

Without this process—and the discipline to stick with it—you might find yourself getting stuck, or worse, losing interest altogether. It's not uncommon for writers to get discouraged and flat-out give up. Some people label this "*writer's block*," but it's likely they simply had no real blueprint for getting through the routine. And, make no mistake, writing is all about routine.

. . .

THE LOGICAL FIRST QUESTION IS: What exactly is a *process*? Followed by: How does it help you go from rough idea to published?

My gut reaction to the second question is to say "*I don't know*." Because, in truth, I don't think anyone knows exactly how this stuff works. But it makes a difference for most writers. Or, more specifically, for most *successful* writers.

In a nutshell—and perhaps overly simplified—a writing process is the marriage of methods with a check-list. The methods include any and all techniques that spur your most productive output, including the quirks that feed your obsessive-compulsive disorder. Yes, if you're a writer, I'm assuming you have your share of OCD tendencies. Good.

The checklist should stretch all the way from how you compile your ideas and your specific notes, to how you schedule your writing sessions, through the steps necessary to publish the finished product.

WE'RE lucky to have a record of the processes used by prolific writers. These in no way should be used as a barometer to measure your own process. It's just useful to know that ten different writers have ten different methods for pumping out words.

Alexander Hamilton, one of the founding fathers, churned out literally millions of words before getting his ass shot by Aaron Burr and winding up as the inspiration for a hip-hop Broadway musical.

Tens of thousands of pages of Hamilton's writings still exist today. Not words, but actual *pages*. There's no way you do that without a process. His, according to biographer Ron Chernow, was to ruminate on an idea during the day, go get a few hours of sleep, then wake up the next day, start guzzling coffee, and sit at his desk for seven or eight hours.

One side effect of this process, it's said, was the need for minimal editing. Apparently his sleeping mind put order to his thoughts and words.

Or he was just a freak.

For a modern-day example, consider Stephen King. He's famous for swimming in loud, head-banging music while he creates. Turn up the Metallica and turn out the words, dude. I couldn't do it that way, but it's his process, not mine.

Other writers have documented their need for solitude (see Chapter Three), extreme quiet, and chamomile tea. Some are only their best while wearing a favorite piece of clothing. Some write in the buff. Whatever makes the magic happen.

It may take you some experimentation to find the perfect quirky combination. But I guarantee you'll figure it out pretty quickly.

THEN THERE'S the second part of the process equation: the checklist. Again, it ain't sexy, but it's just as important as the Metallica and the chamomile.

Here's an example of the checklist/process I used a few years ago for creating a nonfiction title called *Smart Is Cool*.

First, I laid out a somewhat-detailed outline of the main points to be covered. For many of these I then created sub-points that fell under the umbrella of these main topics.

Having or not having an outline is a personal preference. I understand why some fiction writers ignore it. But nonfiction practically demands it, especially if you're crafting a proposal, which you should do, and is, in itself, an outline. If you think you write better while flying blind, go for it. The rest of the process should never be done blindfolded, however.

Next, I lined up my expert guests. Since *Smart Is Cool* relates to education, I interviewed teachers, principals, parents, and former students who had floundered in school before finally getting it.

You want to find the people in your field who will provide the color to your otherwise black-and-white movie. Do all the research to find who they are, where they are, and how to reach them. Ideally, you'll want to do your research in a clump, rather than scattered between actual writing sessions.

Next I planned a writing schedule. At the time it was roughly one to two hours a day, after getting home from the radio show. If you're able to devote a lot of time, great. If you can only write on weekends and during early morning sprints, block out those hours and make them sacred.

Maybe your book will require photos and illustrations for the words you've just produced, either your own or from a hired gun. A traditional publisher will oversee this work, but if you're going the self-published route it's on you.

During off times, I made decisions about who would be doing the following jobs:

Editing: an editor I've worked with many times was available.

Designing (interior and cover): For me, this was two different people for *Smart Is Cool*. In the past I've used one person to do both inside and out, but often you'll break these tasks up.

Printing: In days gone by we used to have to find an actual offset-printing company to churn out a few hundred to several thousand copies of our creations. That meant practically an entire notebook of printers, quotes, shipping costs, and other associated tasks.

Today we're fortunate to have print-on-demand, which saves both time and storage space for inventory. But it still requires research and work, and it demands that you keep good records of how and where you're uploading your manuscript.

Fulfilling: Simply put, this is the packing and shipping of book orders that you might do from your own web site, if this is a route you choose to take. Damn, this is a whole book unto itself.

Promotion/marketing: Again, an entire book. Maybe *three* books.

I kept a white board with these jobs and the dates by which they'd be completed. Or, in the case of fulfilling and marketing, when they'd begin.

Having all of this looking back at me in colorful marker from the white board provided a calming blanket over the whole job of creating the book. Yes, the writing is crucial, but having a process and its checklist in place for building the other components alleviated a measure of stress.

A QUICK SIDENOTE. While you're in the writing phase, don't let others knock you off schedule. Say no to lunch dates or other requests that conflict with your time. You won't be writing this book forever, so graciously tell them why you're saying no for now and offer to reschedule when your book is ready to publish.

NOW YOU SEE why the majority of a writing life is unsexy. It's serious work, but the average reader doesn't see all the crap going on behind the curtain. When your book comes out they'll simply notice the cover and the words.

Your writing process is your template for getting to the finish line. It cradles your rough idea, supporting it through all the steps required to birth a book out of a manuscript.

More importantly, it fends off discouragement. When we lose sight of what's next, when we get lost in—or over- whelmed by—the variety of chores we need to knock out, we get down on the entire effort. Writing ceases to be fun and becomes aggravating.

Forget about goals, and instead focus on systems. Mine may not work for you, and yours could be alien to me. If you're like me, though, and you have no "average" day of writing because of full-time work and other responsibilities, your system may involve literally scheduling time to write. And I do mean putting it in your calendar. Regardless, find and develop your process, even if it changes over time. Your work will be better, and your writing life will be smoother and hopefully easier.

12

BORED

People are often surprised to learn that I'm an introvert. *"But you're a morning radio show host,"* they say. *"How can you possibly be an introvert?"*

I like to say I'm an introvert who pretends to be an extrovert. That approach serves me well in a professional sense. I can fake it. Besides, radio is my escape. We all need one, and those four hours in the studio provide mine.

A poll of my fellow seventh-grade students would likely have declared me the least likely to do anything in show business, which is what good morning radio is. We associate entertainers with an outgoing personality, people who crave the spotlight. But I was a shy kid, often almost painfully so. My sister made friends in a heartbeat, while I hung back, observing. So I spent a lot of time alone with my own thoughts.

This isn't a plea for sympathy. Quite the contrary. I wouldn't go back and change a thing, because this solitary stretch seeded my creative field.

Okay, so it sounds like confected crap, but I'm convinced my background contributed to my writing, and in a big way. Because as a kid I learned how to be bored. And that, in turn, fired up my creativity.

This chapter is an ode to the *beauty* of boredom. As a writer, especially a writer who may often feel stymied by the challenges of producing a finished product and getting it to market, boredom not only is your friend, but possibly your savior.

FOR WHATEVER REASON, people are enamored with the genesis of story ideas. Every author who's ever published a story has fielded the question, "*Where did you get the idea?*" This assumes that stories are born in some abstract, faintly-mystical zone, one that's accessible only by a select few.

The truth is much less romantic. Stories are born from boredom.

When did boredom become such a wicked thing? Why do we work so hard to eliminate even the chance of being bored? And what do we have to do to convince people to stop fighting it and actually embrace boredom?

The antidote, we tend to believe, is some form of distraction. And holy shit, the distraction industry is worth billions and billions of dollars. (See earlier chapter.) There are entire industries built around the task of occupying your poor, starving mind, the one that must have something to occupy it.

You pay people to distract you, often so you won't be —gasp!—bored. But if you have dreams of becoming a published author, it would be wise to shift that thinking. Boredom, you see, is the breeding ground for bestsellers.

Today, we don't allow ourselves to be bored. Between streaming TV, social media, YouTube, and the ever-present phone, there's an endless stream of noise and pictures assaulting us. Ever watch people when they get into an elevator? Heaven forbid we stand still for twenty-three seconds without pulling out our digital babysitter.

Continually shoving prefabricated bullshit content into your head doesn't leave any room to develop your own creativity. And the people who sell that content wouldn't have it any other way.

I grew up in a fortunate time for stimulating creativity. Without access to anything digital, I spent countless hours outside, playing and exploring, allowing my introverted mind to fill in a lot of gaps. By nature we fill in these gaps with fantasies, creating scenarios and adventures, big and small, that entertain us and sharpen our senses.

What about you? You're reading this because you likely have a desire to create words and then distribute those words to the world. How much room are you leaving for daydreaming, for speculating, for mindlessly wandering?

Are you filling your spare time—whatever that is for you—with someone else's content? Are you allowing your senses to absorb every nuance around you?

There's not a day in the year where I don't invest at least one hour outside, walking through the park nearby. Sometimes I'll listen to a podcast or an audiobook. But most of the time it's quiet, only the breeze and the wildlife touching my senses. No artificial sounds whatsoever.

And my mind goes hog wild. You have no idea how many story ideas, blog post ideas, and general publishing ideas have sprung from those walks. My phone's note section is crammed with these thoughts. Sometimes I'll quickly type them into a folder, or I'll record a voice-note while walking. Then the phone is stored again and the slate is once again blank. Most people would describe that hour as boring. It's not. It's magical.

WHEN IT CAME time to edit this chapter, I stumbled onto an idea. What if I considered not only my bibliography of completed books, but also scanned the files of story ideas I've kept for years. How many of them, I wondered, can pinpoint their genesis to an event that happened in the midst of people and activity, versus those that leapt from my bored mind?

Each of the 10 novels I've published so far developed during quiet time. Of my three middle grade books, two of them can trace their origin to a discussion or interaction with someone. The other was born alone.

My first collection of short fiction has six entries. Five of the six were boredom-induced. One came from a happy hour outing.

A three-book young adult mystery series has two finished manuscripts and one partial. All three came about because of hikes. Even if I was hiking with another person, I didn't discuss the books. They evolved during quiet time in nature.

Suggestions for a follow-up series to my *Galahad* books came from emails and book-signing encounters with readers. So those go in the non-bored column.

But 22 other novel and short story ideas—the ones that have lengthy notes in my computer—grew from solitude.

That's forty-four stories (novels and short fiction). Four of them owe their inspiration to people and sound. That's nine percent. The other ninety-one percent—in other words, the vast majority—would never have happened if it wasn't for boredom.

STOP FEARING THE BOREDOM BEAST. A mind that doesn't have shit pumped into it must find something to focus upon, and that's where creativity blooms. When you find yourself with downtime—even if it's just your commute to and from work—embrace it, don't shun it. Ignore your digital devices. When you have an opportunity to get outside, especially away from traffic, grab it. Treasure it.

If you want to create interesting stories, and if you're serious about seeing them through to publication, I urge you to shut out all of the artificial stimuli and immerse yourself in quiet. Be bored. And be bored for long stretches, not just four minutes.

It's difficult to fill a container that's already full.

13

HORSE

Welcome to the world where promotional hype is the media's supernova, outshining everything else. It was perfected by the major television networks, pimping their sitcoms and sporting events, to the point where it seems we watch more promos than actual programming. Today, though, it has trickled down and permeates just about every creative outlet in the country. And, with the explosion—and undeniable power—of social media, it's easier than ever to hype a message to thousands—sometimes millions—with a click or two.

But an important ingredient is often left out of the cake that eager authors are trying to bake: good words.

Bob Mayer touched on this in his excellent blog, found at BobMayer.com. In March of 2012, while sharing some thoughts on the proliferation of ebooks, he counseled enthusiastic authors to remember the most important element of a successful book, regardless of format—and it's not the promo video on YouTube.

It's the actual content of the book.

Each month I receive a dozen or more questions about writing and publishing from people who are anxious to put out a hit book. But I find at least half of those requests focus exclusively on how often they should Tweet, or how I set up my Facebook page, or how many times I send out a newsletter blast.

In other words, a fascination with social media—coupled with countless news stories about yet another viral success—has too many writers not only putting the cart before the horse, but leaving the poor horse tethered in the barn. They're trying to magically roll the cart into town with gimmicks.

When I respond to these questions with information about the writing process itself or by asking how many hours a day they dedicate to composing meaningful and melodious paragraphs, I hear crickets. Few writers, it seems, are interested enough in the nuts and bolts. Instead it's all about "*how can I blast a billion eyeballs with my snazzy promo video?*"

The poor horse is waiting.

DON'T MISUNDERSTAND. You need to be good at spreading the word about your words. In fact, if you're not willing to work that aspect of the business, you might as well consign yourself to writing as a hobby. And there's nothing wrong with that.

But, on the flip side, peddling garbage is more than a little dangerous. If you're able to convince a million people to check out your story by using flash and pizzazz, ultimately they'll still judge you by your writing—with some famous exceptions that will go unnamed.

In other words, when you finally secure those eyeballs, the payoff better be worth it, because you'll never fool them again. They'll remember your name, and for the wrong reason.

YOU MIGHT CONSIDER this dated advice, a vain attempt to stem the tsunami of super-hype continually flooding us. Viral videos rule the day, and that won't end anytime soon. Sure, I watch them, too. I might hate myself for wasting precious time on the brain's equivalent of junk food, but I'm human. And cats are fucking hilarious.

Without a doubt, it's easier to conceive a silly two-minute video than to craft an 80,000-word novel. And it's fiendishly alluring to imagine an army of people Malcolm Gladwell, in his book *The Tipping Point*, coined "Connectors," rabidly sharing your work with the masses. These trendsetters are often responsible for hit books, songs, movies, gadgets, and fashion. And we have no idea who they are. They're faceless, nameless creatures of influence, powerful as hell but practically anonymous.

So what are the odds you'll be blessed by the touch of the Connectors? Especially when thousands of other writers are courting them at the same time?

Some authors actually purchase email lists or social media "friends." They begin force-feeding promotional pitches and flat-out advertising at these innocent souls, people who had no idea the author even existed until they got an email alert. And then another.

Yes, social media is an important tool. Building a database of readers and fans can be a critical component of your marketing plan. But it must—it *must*—be secondary to the delicate creation of your craft.

Marketing shit to millions of people only establishes you as one very determined shit-shoveler. Marketing solid, thoughtful prose builds a reputation that will serve you beyond your first book, through your second, on to your third.

MY ADVICE IS to dedicate the bulk of your time and energy to perfecting your writing skills, and then to use your *spare* time polishing your social media marketing. While I might question Anders Ericsson's 10,000-hour rule (made famous in another of Gladwell's books, *Outliers*), I can't deny his basic premise regarding practice. Work each day to become better and better, and always aim to make your next manuscript better than the last one.

No one remembers a damned thing about Harper Lee's marketing. Did she even have any?

14
———————

STUDENT

C an you teach someone to write well?

Are we born with an intrinsic ability to craft words, or can we be schooled into the art? Both?

This theme was the subject of a semi-heated debate I witnessed at a writing conference. I remained mute on the issue, choosing instead to watch everyone else make a fool of themselves.

Because they don't know the answer. Nor do you. I don't either, although I have a guess, like everyone else. The question involves one of those endless-loop arguments that allows people to puff themselves up. I've written on the subject, but only to the extent that I find the science element interesting.

To me it boils down to four simple words: *Who gives a shit?*

If you want to write, if you want to tell your personal story, or take people on a dark, winding journey through your warped imagination, I don't think it matters if you were born with a talent for the work or if you studied your ass off to learn it.

The reason I'm bringing it up here is because the *teach-you-how-to-write* industry makes a bundle of loot every year. It probably has pocketed a few dollars that used to belong to you.

FOR THE RECORD, and to be perfectly clear, I am not against people selling you educational books or courses. Not at all. There's a lot of solid information from some talented, experienced teachers.

Alongside the books on writing you'll find books and courses that teach you how to *publish*, which is a little different from how to *write*. Writing is about a craft, the muse, the universe, and such. It springs from a place in your mind that I'll never understand, and I don't need to. To me it just happens.

Publishing, on the other hand, is nuts and bolts, a sequence of steps that has nary an aerie-faerie component within it. You do this, then you do this, and don't forget to do that.

I will, however, counsel you to proceed with caution, for two reasons.

First, be sure the book or course isn't claiming you'll become the next Grisham or Morrison or Tan. You don't need to be the next Toni Morrison. We already have one, and she kicks ass. You need to be the first you.

A truly good book on writing doesn't make promises. Some, in fact, even try to talk you out of doing it, and I'm not kidding. I remember a piece by a bestselling author who basically said, "*Maybe this game ain't for you.*" I considered the author's honesty honorable. I also found it downright hilarious.

What the *best* ones do, really, is guide you through the styles that have worked well in the past. Emphasis on *past*, because who the hell knows what will be considered great writing in another generation?

The stellar *how-to-write* books make you think. Some are penned by bestselling authors, some by noted writing instructors, and some by people who just understand the process. You may already know much of it, but there may be a nugget or two that's new to you.

The second reason you should be cautious of these books is almost ironic, but it's what I most want you to consider before you dive into a library of them. While your intention is to learn and to glean wisdom from the masters, there's a trap in this. Think of it as PSS: Perpetual Student Syndrome.

As with many of the issues I've brought up—or will soon bring up—in this book, I'm guilty as charged. Traditional school may end after the twelfth grade, but as of this writing I'm essentially in the fiftieth grade. I happen to love learning, whether it's technology, history, or science.

This is a damned good way to be, and I applaud you if you're a perpetual learner, too. I have no scientific data to quote, but I personally subscribe to the notion that life-long learners are slower to age and healthier in general. And, to boot, they're just more interesting to be around. They're sure as hell more fun to talk with.

So this is a good thing. Until it's not. And it's *not* when you find yourself fearful of actually *doing something* until you've read all about it, again and again and again. And again.

(And, yes, I do appreciate the humor in the fact that I'm telling you this in a book that some would say is meant to teach you something. Perhaps I'm splitting hairs, but I intended *The Color of Your Dreams* to be more of a helping hand with the mental/psychological side of writing rather than a how-to manual.)

You may have fallen into this trap. It's easy to do, because we tend to always feel like we're *not quite ready* when we take on a life-changing project. And publishing your first book is life-changing.

I tend to over-study everything. I recently bought a new refrigerator, and you'd have thought making the wrong decision meant I'd have a hand cut off. I spent weeks reading reviews and going to look at the various models. I wanted to be right when I finally pulled the trigger. Of course, the fridge could be at the top of the ratings and still be a piece of shit when you get it home.

With publishing we want to tread softly, but tiptoeing isn't always the best advice. You can be way too careful. The world's most successful entrepreneurs started their businesses before they even really knew what they were doing. They dove in, they quickly learned from their missteps, and they course-corrected. In the business world it's known by the cutesy phrase "*ready, fire, aim.*"

When it's time to publish your book or start your blog or your podcast, you can learn the basics pretty quickly. You don't need to keep reading and rereading other tales of success. And, if you're going to be publishing ebooks, there's a wonderful thing called "edit-and-resend." You can correct a mistake in a digital book in less than five minutes.

All of this has (or should have) forward momentum. When you finish one book, you begin the next. And it will be better. When you post your first podcast, you begin work on the next. Which will also be better.

You probably know this, and yet you *still* keep reading multiple books about writing. I've got news for you: This is one of those cases where we truly learn by doing. Reading about writing is like reading about sex. The chapters may be stimulating, but it's way more fun to just do it.

HERE'S my recommendation if you're stuck in this tar pit. Find a ratio of reading and writing that provides enough support while nudging you into creative mode. I don't know what that ratio is, but you might start with three-to-one. Spend three times as many hours actually doing the work for every hour you spend studying it.

Because you should never stop reading about it. Never. The writers who feel they've mastered the craft are full of it. They're also the writers whose fifteenth book is no better than their first. The sixth and final book of my *Galahad* young adult book series was considerably better than the first. I love them all, but even I recognize that the writing became much better.

We get nervous that we don't know enough to compete. Well, you probably do. Locking yourself into

PPS shows that you're still shackled by insecurity, afraid of fucking up.

News flash, amigo: The only way you truly screw up your writing career is if you rush a book to market that could stand a round of edits, or if you develop a diva attitude. Hard-working, earnest, and humble writers are generally embraced, not just by the reading community but by their peers, too.

JOHN WHEELER, the physicist who's credited with popularizing the term "*black hole*," said: "*We live on an island surrounded by a sea of ignorance. As our island of knowledge grows, so does the shore of our ignorance.*"

AND HE'S RIGHT, of course. The more we learn, the more there *is* to learn. Intellectual curiosity, I'm convinced, is one of the key components in remaining forever young and vital. Just don't make it the *only* component. Actually use the information you're gaining. Go write.

I know you want to keep reading about the life of a writer. The problem is that you're really just living the life of a reader.

15

RELEASE

There's a certain dance competition show on television that—at least as of this writing—snares a fair amount of attention. Various performers from the screen and from the athletic field prance before judges and a rapturous studio audience before receiving a numeric score for their efforts.

It's all quite campy and produced, but it delivers ratings (sigh) so there's undoubtedly more to follow.

Although I'm happy for viewers who wring joy from that hour, personally I don't care about the cast nor the contestants, and dancing itself is just not my taste. We're all different. *C'est la vie* and all that.

There's something they do on the show, however, that flies in the face of my belief system. It draws a thunderous ovation whenever it happens, and people breathlessly send out social media updates trumpeting the event.

They award perfect 10s.

In your world a perfect 10 may be something treasured and revered. In my world they don't exist. Perfect

10s, in my opinion, reside with the unicorns and mermaids.

Yes, it's mostly semantics, and we can debate *perfection* all day. But, to me, perceived perfection breeds complacency. Since I was a teenager, I've always wanted to reach just a little further, aim a little higher, and always have something to shoot for.

If we award ourselves a perfect 10, what is left to achieve?

There's a reason I bring this up.

There's not a story I've written that I didn't want to rewrite. There's not an article I've published that I didn't want to chop up and start from scratch. There's not a chapter in this book that will completely satisfy me.

I'm speaking your language right now, eh?

Writers are rarely happy with their work. Oh, we like the finished product for the most part, and we're thrilled to wrap it up. But ultimately happy? Not usually. It seems we can never find perfection in anything we create. Rare is the writer who is not his or her own worst critic.

Two thoughts here. One, all of this is okay. I say it's okay to beat yourself up—to a point. I swear it will contribute to make you a better writer—to a point.

And here comes thought two. Eventually you have to release your shit to the universe. And the moment you do that, your perfectionist ways have got to stop. Lamenting a project you've finished only damages your delicate writer psyche and prevents you from truly moving on to the next story or article.

Listen, I'm guilty of this, and that's why I'm qualified to speak about its evils. I've held on to stories that were allegedly finished years ago. With each of them there's something—and often I can't quite put my finger on what it is—that screams "*This isn't ready!*" I always long to tinker.

If you deconstruct the issue, it's hurting you in a couple of ways. It's reinforcing some bullshit notion that you're not good enough, and—this is much more important—it's distracting you when you should be on to your next piece.

WE DREAM BIG. We imagine literary success, however you choose to define it, and we compare ourselves to other writers. Constantly. But you'll note we never compare ourselves to shitty writers, or even mediocre scribes who publish yet sell only a handful of books. No, we hold our work up to the giants in the industry, or at least to those who make a lot of money with their words.

And that's okay, as long as it's not hobbling your craft.

My first novel was a regional hit, and it had some notable achievements. The American Library Association named it one of their Top Shelf picks, alongside some little book called *The Hunger Games*, which I've heard did pretty well.

All of this after I spent almost a year fretting that there was so much more I could've done to make the story better.

To this day I don't see that book as anywhere near perfect. In some respects I cringe at parts of it, which is ridiculous, because it was a fine little story.

· · ·

MAYBE YOU'RE THINKING about taking baby steps, and instead of trying to land the big fish—a contract for a novel from a prestigious publisher—you're interested in fishing in a smaller pond for now. You'd like to submit a short story to one of the many magazines or superblogs.

I wholeheartedly cheer this decision. Magazines have been fertile ground (sorry to switch metaphors) for many of the biggest names in writing. If you have some misguided notion that this is somehow beneath you, that it's a Big Five contract in New York or nothing, you're crazy. Check out the resume of people like Stephen King, Margaret Atwood, and Gabriel Garcia Marquez. And a ton of others. Their work has graced numerous magazines.

I've submitted to magazines, and you know what? It stirs up the exact same anxiety you feel when you query an agent or a book publisher. The same insecure bullshit bubbles up, and you will read that 4,000-word manuscript about two hundred times before you hit the submit button. I remember even editing a goddamned story five minutes before I stabbed that button.

See, even if it's not the glorious novel you dream about, you will always have this paralyzing obsession with perfection. You'll re-read and re-read, you'll grimace, and you'll question everything.

But this is not *Dancing With The People You Vaguely Recognize*. There will be no perfect 10. You'll *never* be completely satisfied with your work.

And that's okay.

It means you're a writer.

To be blunt, and to bring this home, here's what it

boils down to: Screw perfection. That doesn't mean you shouldn't slave away, producing the best work you're capable of. It means you need to give it all you've got, then *let it go*. Release it to the universe, if it helps you to frame it that way. If you don't want to submit it to contests, fine. Just get it out there, somewhere, somehow.

The more you do this, and the sooner you learn to give your all to a manuscript before that sweet release, the sooner you'll be on to your next piece.

Which will probably be even better.

Unlike a really badass samba (apparently), there has yet to be a book that's a perfect 10.

16

FINISHING

There may not be a soul on the planet better at starting a piece of writing than I am. Novel, short story, article, blog post, I don't care. Once an idea enters my brain, once I even sniff the potential of the work, my neurons begin to fire at an outrageous pace, to the point where I need to quickly scribble down the notes before literary gold (right?) is lost forever.

I'm a prodigious creator of ideas. The funny thing is, for years I wore it like some badge of honor. A friend once gave me a notebook with an embossed plate on the cover that read "*Idea Man*." Seriously.

Sound familiar? Did I just describe you?

If so, allow me to suggest something that may deflate your pride a bit, just as it did my own. *Having a shitload of ideas isn't worth much, if anything.*

Yes, you can brag about it, as I did. You can sit alone at your writing table and puff out your chest about your badass ideas. But here's the truth: Nobody retires on their book ideas. Yeah, if there was a *USA Today* chart of the

Top 50 Book Ideas, there's a good chance you'd see my name peppering that list. There isn't, and you won't.

GREAT STARTERS ARE COMMONPLACE. Great finishers are rare. What will it take for you to move along the path from inspired idea, to solid start, to strong finish? How do you stay resolute in your desire to see the entire project through to publication?

Once you pen the final word, the steps necessary to actually get your work out into the universe are not that complicated. Somewhat intimidating, sure, but nothing you can't manage. So the monkey wrench here is the speed bump that has slowed your writing pace and threatened your *The End*.

Again, I can cover this topic because I've lived it. Goddamn, have I lived it. My laptop's documents folder testifies to the unfinished work waiting for attention.

But I've also powered through the issue, too. One of the most daunting tasks I've faced was finishing a six-book young adult series, and delivering every manuscript to Tor Books by their deadline. Languishing over the final product wasn't an option. Well, I guess it *was* an option if I didn't mind returning my publisher's advance.

I finished that series on time. And I've finished more than a dozen other books, too. So let's talk about finishing.

I'VE ALREADY COVERED distractions in another chapter, and those often play a significant role in our inability to wrap things up. Let's assume, though, that your phone is shut down, the TV is off, and you're dutifully sitting in front of your screen, ready to create. Mostly ready to create. The spirit is willing, you know, but the words remain stubbornly unwritten. It's like shy bladder syndrome. You've really gotta pee, but . . .

Two primary culprits loom here, and the first is pure insecurity. You just don't believe in your words, and you don't believe you can pull off the grand finale.

Listen, this is such a common affliction, and it's So. Damn. Dumb.

You're worried that you're not going to do your book justice, so you sit there, paralyzed, over-analyzing not just the ending but likely the entire piece. You may love what you've banged out so far, but the ending is murky and frightening.

Yeah, okay. It can be *very* frightening. And you could conceivably rewrite the ending a few times, maybe second-guessing every word. Maybe you end up with a final chapter that doesn't produce an orgasm, but it's probably not nearly as bad as you think.

And what's worse: having an ending that doesn't launch a magnificent pyrotechnic display, or a manuscript that makes it to the eighty-two percent mark before petering out?

Don't misunderstand this. I never advocate for rushing through something just to say you did it. We all can spot the book that was mindlessly thrown together, an obvious attempt at a cash-grab. We're not talking about that. If this subject resonates with you, it's because you're thoughtfully concerned about the quality of your work. Thank you for that dedication.

Just don't let it hobble you.

One other thought on this. Stop for a moment and think about some of the best authors you've read. Now think about each of their books, and tell me that you sincerely believe every single one of them had a stellar ending.

Not happening, is it?

One of my all-time favorite writers, who will, for obvious reasons, go unnamed, makes a habit (in my opinion) of shitty endings. One that jumps to mind was so bad that I almost threw the book across the room. I know a "*You've got to be fucking kidding me!*" sprang from my mouth.

But this writer also has enough clever, just-right endings to salvage his/her image in my mind. I don't see a new title hit the bookstore and think, "*Nope, too many bad endings.*" I buy the work because I think the writing is (in general) interesting, entertaining, and often thought-provoking. The books just (sometimes) suck at the end.

I had to laugh when I heard that author Cormac McCarthy allegedly said, "*A finished book never lives up to its ideal.*"

So goddamned true. Stop with this over-critical assessing at all times. Give it your best shot, try multiple drafts with a little experimentation thrown in, and get to *The End*.

Then get on with the next project.

. . .

THE OTHER ROADBLOCK is the fear of what to do next. I recently had a conversation with a woman who told me she loved to write, but she'd never do anything with that passion because the thought of having to publish something was overwhelming.

I'll give her this much: The road to publication *used to be* overwhelming. For that matter, it used to be humiliating most of the time. You'd have to crawl to an agent, or crawl to a publisher, and their numerous rejections made you question whether you had even an ounce of talent.

Again, I've been there. It hurts. It sucks. And it does create doubt in your abilities, even if the brush-off was simply a case of reaching an editor's assistant on one of their crappy days. You'll never know, right?

(I did what other writers have done and kept many of the rejection notices. For some reason, most of us can't resist the "*I'll show you*" mentality. Hey, whatever motivates you to get it done, right?)

This is one of the reasons I use social media to share my thoughts on the entire process; it's why I created this book. Not because I'm a writing guru who can show you how to produce perfect prose, but because I hate to see people with a genuine talent in writing and a sincere interest in publishing get the shaft from The Man. (That's just a saying, by the way; chances are the shaft will actually come from a woman. They seem to dominate the world of words as agents, editors, and publishers.)

The truth is, it's just not that tough to get your words out there. Whether in ebook form or good ol' traditional print, the steps to go from finished manuscript to published volume are substantially easier than when I put out my first book.

People generally haven't received this memo, however. And maybe the large publishing houses prefer you never get the damned memo, although I don't subscribe to the suspicion that these heavyweights are trying to shut down *all* independent publishing. I think they're legitimately trying to protect the integrity of the industry by limiting the amount of crap that's foisted on the public. (That's another topic for another time.)

We're quickly approaching the time, I believe, when more eager writers will realize the calling is no longer reserved for the anointed few. As more people grasp the tools and the techniques for publishing, the mystique will dissolve.

Be aware that you'll always encounter snobs who condemn the idea of mass publishing. Personally, I say fuck them and their word bigotry. I've read some of the things they laud as evolved, exceptional writing, and it often gives me the runs. Then some poor, abused indie writer will put out a masterpiece.

If you've been held back because you're unsure of how to take the next steps, that excuse has officially been shattered. Besides, regardless of how easy or difficult it is to get the words out there, you need to have them written anyway, if for no other reason than the pride you'll feel at finishing.

Baby steps, my friend. Write the story/essay/article/post, make it the best it can be through multiple drafts, have it professionally edited (unless it's a casual blog post, where that might be overdoing it a tad). Make it shine. Then give it wings.

The instructions on how to do that last part are available in many places, shared by people who've done it many times. Just find those instructions wherever you can, and show us your work.

Finish what you started.

17

SUBMITTING

I t's easy to fall into the mind trap that you haven't arrived as a writer until you've either sold a ton of books, made the *Times* list, collected tens of thousands of blog/social media followers, or won awards for your words.

We mistakenly believe these landmarks are the only yardsticks by which to measure achievement. But there's another step on the ladder of success that's easily within your grasp. In fact, I think it's worth two or three steps because of the effect it has on your spirit.

It's best illustrated with a story.

YOU MIGHT THINK WINNING an international grand prize from *Writer's Digest* changed my life, but no. Sealing and stamping an envelope is what changed everything.

Don't get me wrong, the award was—and still remains —a tremendous honor, and I'm thankful to the magazine and its editors for the selection. The notation in my bio adds credibility, a cachet that's priceless for a writer's marketability. But if you're struggling with the decision of participating in a writing contest, let me give you a different perspective.

I was forty-four years old when I won the award for my young adult novel, *The Comet's Curse*, but I'd been writing since junior high school, always just for fun. I'd never once submitted a story of any length to any agent, to any publisher, or to any contest. Writing was my little secret, something I occasionally shared with a close friend. Usually, however, the pages wound up in a manilla folder, tucked into a drawer.

Then one day I read a portion of what would become *The Comet's Curse* to a classroom of sixth-graders. Now *that's* pressure. But when they enthusiastically cheered and demanded to know when they could read it all, I finally bypassed the folder and set about publishing a book. I did my homework, learned to use special publishing software, hired an editor, the works. Roughly a year later I held my first novel in my hands.

It was my son who said, "*Writer's Digest has an international contest for writing. You should send in your book.*"

Initially I snorted. After years of writing in secret, toiling away to merely entertain myself, I thought the suggestion was ridiculous. Then I reconsidered. I decided that Writer Dom needed to grow a set. A week later the book was in the mail.

I came to the conclusion that submitting your writing to a contest is not much different than reading your work to a group of tough-to-please eleven year olds. It's about getting beyond the *hobby* mentality and recognizing that your writing does no good in a drawer.

There are great singers who never perform in front of anyone. There are talented painters who have filled their closets and basements with canvases that no one has seen. And then there are writers.

By nature, artists are shy, sometimes painfully so. We live to create, but too often we don't truly *believe* in those creations. Because we admire and often revere the writers we follow, we consider ourselves unworthy of print, unable to measure up to their standards.

Which is bullshit. Your calling is to write, not to imitate. Nobody said anything about measuring your words against those of the greats, or against anyone else, for that matter. And remember, the writers you worship had writers *they* adored, too. What if your hero had decided she wasn't worthy? What if she had stashed all of her work in manilla folders?

Or maybe you think your words don't need to be delivered to the masses. More than one person has asked me for publishing advice and then added, "*But I don't need to write a bestseller. This is just for my family and friends.*"

Well, there's nothing wrong with that, I suppose. I was a hobbyist for a long time, too. But my thinking changed with the unexpected success of my first book. I had no intention of writing a hit. But look at it this way: If you're going to put that much time and hard work into your art, what harm could there be in sharing it with the universe? Why automatically assume that no one will enjoy it? What if they were *waiting* for it? Even just one person, someone you'll never meet?

I'm not big on memes, and you won't see me posting inspirational sayings on social media. But one of my favorite quotes holds an important lesson for all of us:

"The world is not served when you think small."

I SUBMITTED MY BOOK. And I won. I'll never forget the phone call from Chuck Sambuchino from *Writer's Digest*, and his opening sentence: "*Dom, if you're driving right now, you should probably pull over.*"

(Chuck, by the way, is one of the best people in the business. He's not only a successfully published author, editor, and musician, but someone who has helped countless people on their path to publishing. Check him out at ChuckSambuchino.com.)

But here's the thing, and I mean this sincerely. My writing life didn't change when I won the award from *Writer's Digest*. It changed when I *submitted* the book to their editors. *That* was the turning point, because when you're ready to submit your work, you've crossed the threshold from tinkerer to creator, from hobbyist to artist.

IN SCHOOL we were admonished to show our work. Although it's a different context, the principle still applies. You've invested not only time, but chunks of your *soul*, for chrissakes. You believed enough in the words to transfer them from your mind onto a screen, and hopefully into print.

Please don't banish those words to a folder.

(I just recently stumbled across a book about this notion by a guy named Austin Kleon. He calls it, fittingly, *Show Your Work!* He's essentially asking you to be brave, and that's really what it boils down to.)

Sending away your work to be judged is the step that profoundly alters your writing mind for good. It's your coming out, your one-small-step that identifies you as a writer, even if it's celebrated alone.

When you actually attach that document file and hit *submit*, you're taking a giant leap. You're taking a chance. You're stepping off that ledge and trusting that, even if you don't soar like a majestic eagle, you won't tumble to the ground.

Hey, you might never win the prize. But you win, nonetheless.

18

DESIRE

You've been ambushed outside a grocery store by the world's smallest salespeople, right? Girl Scouts, Boy Scouts, soccer teams, and other little tykes with bottomless supplies of goodies to sell. Usually something that will make you fat, but in the most delicious way.

My co-workers on the morning radio show gave me endless shit when I told a story about one of my encounters with Scouts. The kids were selling chocolate bars for their troop, and approached every store customer with the same high-pitched pitch: *"Hey, wanna buy a candy bar?"*

I stopped and, with the parents listening, said, *"How would you like to double your sales?"* Of course, heads bobbed excitedly.

"Then stop asking people," I said, *"to* buy *anything. I don't care how good it is, never say 'Wanna buy?' Instead, try a new approach. Say, "You know what would be perfect tonight after dinner? One of these delicious chocolate bars. You*

could have half of it tonight, and eat the other half on your way to work tomorrow. It's so good!"

Sure, you can roll your eyes at me coaching twelve-year-olds. Whatever. I guarantee you they doubled their freakin' sales after that. Nobody wants to *buy* anything, including you. You may like to shop, you may like eating and collecting stuff, but the average person inherently hates the question, *"Wanna buy?"*

But they do love their chocolate. For the benefit of the snot-nosed Scouts, we built an image in the minds and taste buds of their customers.

We created *desire.*

IN A BROADCASTING CAREER beginning when Jimmy Carter was in office, I've produced thousands of commercials. Not hundreds. Thousands. Additionally, the number of commercials I've simply played during my radio shows has topped the half-million mark. I've essentially listened to more than half-a-million attempts by companies to sell their products. I know a thing or two about the process.

Which is why I'm astounded at the number of shitty commercials that abound. I wanna scream, *"You had one job! Make me want to buy your product!"*

That's really at the core of the best product pitches ever. You don't want to sell something. You want to create desire. The customer will do the rest of the work for you. As some old ad agency crank said years ago, they'll beat a path to your door.

There's a special application of this principle for

creative types, so if you're a writer, blogger, or video-star-wanna-be, stay tuned.

When I speak professionally on advertising to agencies and companies, we talk about this desire. Because although some people swear that everyone hates advertising, I disagree. They hate *shitty* advertising. But if I love Taylor Swift (or Metallica—the artist doesn't matter), and you play a commercial telling me that she/they have a concert in the park coming up in two months, I wanna know about it. You play clips of my favorite songs, and I have a desire to go see the live show. I don't say, "*God, I hate commercials.*" I want you to tell me how to get the tickets.

All you have to do is rephrase your pitch into a benefit for me, not for you. Or for Taylor. Have you noticed that you've never heard one concert commercial that said, "*Wow, Taylor Swift sure would like for you to come to her show?*"

No. They stir the emotion of anticipation, with sounds of cheering crowds, people losing their minds because everyone—everyone—wants to see this goddess of pop music. "*Oh, my God, you're a complete loser if you don't wanna see this show!*"

This is where independent creative folks, including writers, generally drop the ball. I can't tell you how many authors I've seen on Facebook saying, "*I'm selling copies of my new book. Buy yours at myfreakingbook.com.*"

Repeat with me: Nobody wants to *buy* anything. But they do want stuff, as long as it connects with them and provides a benefit for them. And that's where you, as a book merchant, step in.

When I put my set of *Mindbender* books on sale three times each year, I might position the pitch like this:

"Finding a great gift for Father's Day seems impossible. But he loves to feel smart, right? Save yourself the embarrassment of another Home Depot gift card, and surprise him with The Mindbender books."

Or:

"Stocking stuffers are tough because a lot of things are either too big for a stocking or too expensive. But Mindbender books fit the stocking and your budget (look, they're on sale right now for $5). What if you were finished with your shopping today?"

No ad is perfect, including mine, and you'll never convert everyone. So what? Your goal is to convert *many* of them, not all of them. And step one is addressing their needs, not yours.

Continually asking your friends to support your dream of being a published author won't get you much, especially since social media is easy to hide behind. *"Oh, you had a book signing?"* they say. *"I must've missed that post."*

They didn't miss the post. They saw the post, and they ignored the post, because all you told them was *"I wanna sell a lot of books. If you love me, stop by."*

You know this is true, because your co-workers have sold their kids' shit around the office for years. And you hate it.

. . .

IF YOUR BOOK IS FICTION, it's a little tougher to craft your pitch in a desirable way, but it's still very doable. How about:

"Your son may have said he doesn't like to read, but he just hasn't found the right book. The new adventure story, Nightmare Speedway, *will turn him on to books because it's fun and fast-paced. It was written to appeal to reluctant readers."*

I have yet to meet a parent who isn't anxious for their kids to read. And the issue of reluctant readers, especially among young boys, is real and frightening.

To allay one of your concerns about this approach: This isn't manipulative. Or it is, but not in a deceitful way. Parents *do* want their sons to read, and *Nightmare Speedway* might be one badass, fun book aimed at boys. There sure as hell isn't anything wrong with connecting those dots. You're scratching an itch. What if your book changes a non-reader into a reader?

If your new novel is historical fiction, find the cool angle that could appeal to a segment of your sphere.

"You think there's a lot of sex scandals in politics today? It's nothing compared to what went on at the founding of our country. Now imagine a beautiful woman who actually used her sexual talents to intentionally bring down an entire political party—and almost an entire country. That juicy tale is at the heart of Founder's Fornication, *which is available on your phone or tablet right now. No one has to know you're reading it."*

The only stupid thing in there is the ridiculous title I dreamed up. But that's a sales pitch that does two things: addresses the public's love of sex and scandal, and assures them they can read it in private.

And nowhere did it use the words "*sell*" or "*buy*." It created desire. Maybe not as much as the horny founders apparently had, but still.

THE NEXT TIME you think about asking your social media friends to support your book, stop and examine the way you're asking. Is there something in it for *them*? Is there a tangible benefit to them putting down $5 or $10 or $25 for your work? What is their desire? How do you tap into it?

Selling books is damned tough. In fact, in a non-scientific survey of aspiring writers I did within the last year, "how to sell" was far and away the number one concern, with 82% of people listing it. That's six times as many check marks as the segment on "how to write." Six times! I get it. I've been selling books to people for a long time, and it's not easy. Nor is it my favorite part of the job. Creating desire, however, at least makes it easier.

Now go out and touch those emotions, sell a bunch, and then reward yourself with that goddamned chocolate bar the Scouts are peddling. Because they're not going away.

19

INSPIRE

For years, besides the other hats I wear as radio host and writer, I've been a professional speaker. All that really means, when you get right down to it, is that I stand on a stage, spew some words, and then an important person in the crowd walks over and hands me a check. Cool gig if you can get it.

The topics I cover include writing, advertising your business, customer service, and, as odd as it may sound, speaking. Yes, people pay me to speak about speaking.

When someone finds out that professional speaking is part of my resume, they often say, "*Oh, so you're a motivational speaker.*"

I cringe every time. Sorry, I know that hundreds of speakers have that term on their websites and business cards, but I think it's nonsense. Overlooking the fact that even the words "*motivational speaker*" sound like the cheesiest bullshit in the world, is that even possible? I mean, can another person actually motivate you to get off your ass and do something?

This is simply my opinion, but if you can't motivate yourself to accomplish something, how can a total stranger, usually with too much product in their hair, mix some lively stories with some bad puns and suddenly alter your course?

I believe it's, at the very most, a short-lived effect caused by dynamic stage skills. There's no denying some of these women and men can command an audience. I've seen them, and they're like wizards.

But are you equally motivated two days later, after the buzz has worn off? I guarantee you the speaker's check lasts a lot longer.

One of my all-time favorite lines says it all:

"MOTIVATION IS *what we look for in order to start something we don't really wanna do.*"

SOUND ABOUT RIGHT?

Oh, man, I gotta get motivated to clean out the garage.

I need to get motivated to workout every day.

If I could just get motivated to lose those fifteen pounds.

THAT'S MOTIVATION. If you don't have it in you, no speaker or book is going to pump it into your system. Your goal is to find ways to motivate yourself to do something, and I believe you have to really want to do it before you can even try.

A friend of mine is a hypnotherapist. She told me that

it's pointless for someone to make an appointment with her if they really don't want to stop smoking. Or if they really don't want to break up with someone. Or lose weight. Or whatever.

The same thing, I believe, applies with motivation when it comes to your words. If you don't want to invest a year of your life into writing, editing, formatting, printing, marketing, and selling your novel, you won't, regardless of what I say in these pages. As the old sports saying goes, you gotta want it.

Do you want it?

INSPIRATION, on the other hand, is different. Inspiration comes from another place, a place we probably will never understand. It's what truly moves us, often on a spiritual level. Even the words—spirit, inspiration—are connected, and were born from a Latin phrase that means "*to breathe.*"

Which, on a side note, we don't do enough. We don't stop, take a deep breath, and evaluate the truth behind all the noise around us. Stress and frustration often block us from realizing what's happening, what's possible, and what we're accomplishing.

Other people, you see, can inspire us. They're usually not standing on a stage when they do it. We're inspired by seeing someone complete a task that seemed Herculean or observing a person's dedication to their work or their calling.

We're (sometimes) inspired by watching a parent quietly go about the thankless job of working while raising a family. They don't stand up at the end of the evening and say, "*You can do this!*" They're not motivational speakers. They're inspiring individuals.

HERE'S why I bring all this up. Another person, even a complete stranger, *can* inspire you to write. You likely have writers who not only awed you while entertaining you, but who inspired you on some level.

Their words touched your spirit, maybe subtly shifting the way you thought about something. Maybe they ignited a desire within you that was always there but needed the fuel this writer provided.

I can name at least three who changed my life. Two of them did it through dedication to their art. I don't know, I guess you could just tell from reading their words that they'd tapped into some mystery zone. They have the spirit for writing I admire so much, that impels me to take up the craft.

The third writer I referenced undoubtedly has that connection to the mystery zone, too, but he actually inspired the shit out of me when his intention was to do the opposite. Truth. It's my favorite writing story ever.

Almost thirty years ago famed writer Harlan Ellison spoke at the University of Denver. A fan of his work, I snagged a ticket, grabbed my worn copy of *Shatterday*, one of his short story collections, and headed to the auditorium.

Ellison spoke for almost two hours, a presentation packed with insight and valuable information on the business of writing. He regaled the crowd with anecdotes spanning his thirty-odd years of crafting stories. I, along with everyone else, chuckled at his frequent rants regarding the people who had wronged him over the years. I think we all knew of his reputation for being, shall we say, a bit cantankerous and more than a little abrasive, but he was on fire that evening.

Imagine my surprise when I soon found myself on the receiving end of his fury.

At the conclusion of his talk, Harlan Ellison sat down to sign books and a huge throng of admirers gathered about. He was personable and chatty as he signed, obviously in a pretty good mood. For him. Until it was my turn at the table.

I was thirty years old, a closet writer, and longed to be published. Here before me was a legend, one who'd inspired me to get serious and to work harder. I was nervous, wondering what to say to this word god. I didn't want to sound like a fool, but I also didn't want to waste this one opportunity to connect with him.

He looked up at me, pen poised, awaiting instructions for the inscription, and I blurted out, *"Would you please write a word of encouragement for an aspiring writer?"*

I can't even describe the look of disgust that broke across his face. He sat back and slammed his pen down on the table. With more than two dozen people crowded around, watching and listening, he stabbed a stubby finger toward my face and went off. Paraphrased, it went along the lines of:

"*You* wanna be a writer! Everybody wants to be a writer! Everyone who reads a book suddenly thinks *they* can be a writer! It's bullshit! If I had a dime for every moron who told me they wanna be a writer. Millions of 'em! You listen to me, son, if you have any fucking brains at all you'll give up this bullshit idea and become—I don't know, a plumber. You know how much money plumbers make? '*I wanna be a writer.*' Jesus, another one. I can't believe it."

He must've lectured me for another thirty seconds, spittle shooting from his mouth. All the people standing near the table went completely still and quiet, like a room of Medusa's victims, afraid he'd next direct his ire upon them.

But no. I was the sole target of Mr. Ellison's rage.

The tongue-lashing completed, he picked up his pen, opened my copy of *Shatterday* to the title page, and fulfilled my request for a word of encouragement. He scribbled:

> *A word of encouragement: Become a plumber.*
> *Harlan Ellison.*

THIS IS A TRUE STORY. I still have the book on my bookshelf, in a place of honor.

Let's talk about inspiration here, okay? I have to believe that nine out of ten people would've sulked out of that auditorium, gone home, and thrown away every half-finished story they had lying around. Then maybe gone to a bar.

But I laughed. I sincerely thanked him for his time,

for his advice, and for his signature. Then I went home, worked late into the night, and banged out at least 1,500 words on a short story. It took me a few years, but eventually I signed a six-figure deal with Tor/Forge, and became the published author I'd dreamed of becoming.

HERE'S THE THING: Harlan Ellison was probably right.

For *many* people. Just not for me.

There are millions of frustrated authors, and that means millions of kind souls who won't ever taste the champagne upon signing a book deal. But I never once took his attack personally, and I never once second-guessed my own internal fire.

The way I look at it, Harlan Ellison was just sitting there, waiting for some poor sap to dare ask him for either advice or a pep talk. He was ready, locked and loaded, and I just happened to be the foil. His rant was, in my mind, a shotgun blast, intended for the thirty or more people within earshot. No, it wasn't aimed at me personally.

It was meant for everybody else. For all the people who *say* they want to write, but don't really want to put in the work.

Harlan Ellison never had any intention of inspiring me. He wanted to do the opposite, to save me from a life of hardship if I wasn't truly invested in writing. You could say he did me a favor. Because, really, if I couldn't handle the derision from one cranky old shithead, how would I fare when the entire world responded to my art? As someone told me, it was almost like a test. And I passed.

Are *you* invested? Are you inspired by the writers who move you? Can a cranky old son of a bitch at a writing conference knock you from that path?

Or will every roadblock, every detour, every misstep only fuel your desire that much more? Inspiration is spirit, my friend. I think we're influenced by spirit, not by some cheesy-ass motivational talk.

Recognize what inspires you. More importantly, do everything you can to be an inspiration to others, not through speeches but through your dedication. When others ask you for advice, be giving. Don't be a Harlan.

THERE'S a fun postscript to this story. Not long ago I published a collection of bizarre short fiction I'd hoarded for years. Some of the pieces even dated back to around the time of my encounter with the grump.

When it came time to publish those stories, I chose a new pen name. To honor my landmark moment in the crosshairs of Harlan Ellison, you can find that collection of tales under the name Harlan Plumber.

Hey, he only suggested I *become* one. He didn't say how.

20

HELP

My two careers have two remarkably different attitudes toward competition.

First, there's radio. I began in that industry as an impressionable teenager, and one of the earliest lessons drilled into my brain was beating the competition.

No, wait, that's not exactly right. We weren't encouraged to just win; we were admonished to *destroy* the other radio stations. It wasn't enough to just have higher ratings. As one general manager told me many years ago, "Testa, I want you to whip them so bad they change format within six months."

Then he chomped down on his cigar, pointed to the door of his office, and went back to penning the agenda for his upcoming HOA meeting.

Things have mellowed a bit through the years, but it's still a cut-throat business. A slip in the ratings of just *a tenth of a point* can mean millions in lost revenue, so you damned well better crush the other guys.

And then there's publishing. Specifically, I'm talking about the world of independent publishing. Is there competition? Well, yes, I guess there is, in a way. If someone's book goes to number one and you're down at number 200, sure, you'd like to wriggle your way up there to the top.

But cut-throat? No. In fact, quite the opposite.

I found this out when I self-published my first book in 2004. Growing up as a radio veteran I'd pretty much assumed every industry operated the same way. That meant every author was out to protect their turf, and would do whatever it took to keep anyone else from selling books.

So imagine my surprise when I encountered an established author who said, "Hey, what help do you need?" Then I spoke to another who asked the same thing. Then I was invited to a monthly meeting of an organization made up of indie authors and publishers. And everyone asked the same thing: "What questions do you have?"

After I finished shaking my head, I figured out *why* the two industries are so different.

Radio's market revenue is a pie. That pie can be cut many different ways, but the total is the same, no matter how many slices. So if a market has, for example, $100 million in available advertising dollars, your station is trying to get the biggest slice possible, while the other stations are doing the same.

But it will still be a total of $100 million for that particular year. It's a finite resource.

Publishing is different. Sure, every publisher and

indie author is competing for revenue, but that number fluctuates. If you love to read and you only find six books that turn you on, you'll buy those six. But if you see four other books that look good, you'll buy them, too.

On the other side of that equation: If two authors with dedicated fans each publish two books in one year, their fans will buy them. But if these same authors are really inspired one year and they each put out *three* books, their fans will happily scoop up all three.

In other words, readers rarely put up a hand and say, *Please stop producing books I like.*

With radio, there may be 40 radio stations in a market, but a person can only listen to one of them on Friday morning at 7:30. The others are shut out. If you add five more radio stations, somebody's going hungry.

Writers have figured this out. When you encourage mediocre writers to become *better* writers, that means more good books hit the market. And that means more people are reading. And that means more people are potential customers.

I don't mean this to sound like we're focusing entirely on the money. Yes, that's an important part of it, no doubt. But while radio is an advertising business, writing is an *artistic* outlet. Businesses compete—often fiercely—with other businesses.

Artists (with a few exceptions) generally help other artists. It brings us joy to see someone else find the same success that we did. It's not a zero sum game. Your gain does not mean my loss. It probably means a gain for both of us.

· · ·

It's been almost 20 years since I first published a book, and not a year has gone by that I haven't marveled at what a caring, generous industry it is. There are some cranks (hell, I just told you about one a chapter ago), but there are a lot of kind souls, too.

Now, before you get the wrong idea, let me coach you on etiquette.

It's never a good idea to just send your manuscript to another author and say, *Please stop what you're doing, read this, and tell me what you think*. People are busy, and they can't just drop everything and critique your work. For you it's just one book. But for the person you sent it to, it might be the 10th manuscript they've received from someone that week.

Don't laugh. That happens.

There's a correct way to go about it. There are writer conferences where authors—some of them very successful—will sit on a panel and answer any question you have. You might bump into them in the hall and be able to pick their brain about one specific thing, something they could answer in about 30 seconds.

Don't ever introduce yourself and begin with, *Hey, could you give me some tips?* Nobody on the planet can condense the writing and publishing world into quick tips. It's like asking someone to give you a two-minute tutorial on how to build a nuclear submarine.

Find author groups online. There are tons of them, and you'll discover right away if they're legit or not. You can see the authors who are on there, and then mosey over to Amazon or some other site and do a quick search to see how their career is going.

If you join one of these groups, don't flood the damned thing with 100 questions the first week. Take time to scroll back through earlier topics. Many of these online groups have an index of subjects you can research, all of the pieces written by someone who was once in your shoes and learned along the way.

If you want to learn it all in 24 hours, you're in the wrong field, my friend. This is a long grind. I promise you all the information is out there. All of your questions have answers posted online if you'll take the time to seek them out rather than jumping into someone's face and demanding they school you one-on-one.

Relax, grasshopper.

Now, there will be times when you *do* get a chance for a solo visit. I've had plenty of chats with beginning writers, sometimes over tea, many times over the phone. Can I do them all? Of course not. But I do my best to give back.

Another hot tip: If some author does agree to meet with you for tea or coffee, pick up the check. They're giving you valuable information, gleaned from years and years in the trenches. The least you can do is buy them a freakin' coffee.

I'D STRONGLY URGE you to never ask someone to a lunch meeting. For one thing it's awkward as hell trying to write shit down while you have a plate of rigatoni in front of you. And besides, lunch is too intimate. Just do tea. One hour, max.

. . .

AND THEN THERE'S the most important tip of all: Pass it on.

If you're new to the world of writing and publishing, it all seems a bit overwhelming. At times it feels like you're drinking from the proverbial fire hose, wondering how you'll ever comprehend it all.

But you will. And then you'll probably do it again. Soon you'll be more comfortable with the process. Don't get me wrong, it's still *work*; but with every step you'll gain more experience, and with that you'll develop more confidence.

Just remember that someone might ask *you* for advice some day. I wrote this book because I realized most of the questions I get aren't about the writing itself; the questions are usually about how to get in the right frame of mind. How to get past the fear and the doubt and finally get something published. I wanted to take everything I'd learned about the mind game behind publishing and put it all in one volume.

But people will have questions for you about the various steps. If they ask about your cover designer, share the name of that person or company. If they want to know about the software system you use, tell them what you like about it and what you don't, then offer to share a link to the company's page. If they want to know about your process, explain to them how you structure your day and ask if they've tried the same thing.

And when they tell you how impossible it all seems, and they wonder aloud if they'll ever see the finish line, smile and tell them you used to feel the same way.

Because you did. But now you're a published author. And any little help you can give might make the dream come true for someone else.

That's a great feeling.

AFTERWORD

Thirty-five years passed between my first attempts at writing stories in the third grade and the day a truck pulled up to my house with pristine new copies of my first published book.

When I speak at writing conferences, one point I continuously drive home is: "*Don't do it like that. Don't wait.*"

I'm not naive enough to believe that everyone should attempt to publish their words. Not everyone *wants* to do that, for starters. Plus, for many people the love of writing is fulfilled in the simplest of ways, whether that be a journal, a blog, or just writing long letters to friends.

And, if we're brutally honest, many people just don't have the chops. Which is fine. They're skilled in areas where you and I probably suck.

But then there's you.

Think back to the first story you wrote, or your first attempt at an article or essay. It's almost funny remembering the distinct cocktail of emotions that mixed with each other, from the initial excitement of creating something, to the crushing doubt that you weren't capable, to the creeping realization that you did indeed have some talent.

But you hesitated to do anything with that talent. Chances are you're waiting still. You write, but you discard the words. Or bury them, like I did for those thirty-five years.

Regardless, if you're a voracious reader and you've dabbled in writing, I'm here to kick you square in the ass.

Listen, there are many in the elite writing world who will do everything to hold you down. The traditional publishing world spent years belittling anyone who tried to publish on their own. The term *self-published* was admonished, even vilified, as a repository for shit. In other words, if the big boys didn't deem it worthy of publication, it didn't qualify as real writing.

Thankfully we've reached an era where that condescending attitude is now considered dated and insulting. And remember, I've worked with New York and have nothing but warm appreciation for my publisher's kindness. She and her entire support staff treated me courteously and professionally, and I will always, *always* be grateful for their support. You could one day enjoy a similar experience.

But thousands—perhaps millions—of others have attempted this journey and been rebuffed.

Welcome to the latest golden age of publishing. You're blessed to occupy a time in history where your words can be shared with whomever wants to read them. You no longer *need* the blessing of an editor in New York or London. Your words can be transmitted to literally billions of people.

Today the power doesn't lie exclusively with the traditional publishing houses. It also lies within you. Are you committed to the task? Are you bold enough to bravely share your thoughts, your ideas, your stories with strangers? Are you prepared to work your ass off to get your words out to the universe?

Before you embark on this journey, however, you probably should audit yourself. Not a financial audit. A guts audit.

First, are your words meant for a mass audience? If it's just a family history you want to write for siblings and cousins, you probably don't need to officially publish. You can print up a few dozen copies of the Lipschitz Family History and distribute them. (Although this humble project could, indeed, trigger a desire for something more robust.)

Second, are you prepared to do the work? Publishing is not difficult. It's not easy, either. The way I look at it, it's just enough work to require that you truly be committed to the process. Just enough work, I figure, to keep cranks from flooding the market with complete shit. But anyone with half a brain and full-on desire can follow the necessary steps to publish.

I like the way Honoree Corder put it: "Are you *interested* in this, or are you *committed* to it?"

Third, is this something you can sustain? There's no

law that you have to publish multiple books if you dip your toe into the pool. You may be one-and-done.

But I'll assume that by simply reading this volume you're serious about the idea of writing and publishing. When I sent out a survey to people who were curious about becoming a published author, I asked what each person's ultimate writing plan involved. Three out of four indicated that they envisioned some sort of income from their words, either full-time or simply for extra cash. Only a quarter said their writing would be a hobby and nothing else.

And I can't help but believe a portion of that last group secretly hold out a hope they could do more.

So where does that leave you today? It's possible you've already published one or more pieces. Perhaps you're close, but haven't actually presented your work to the world. Or, just as likely, you've toyed with writing but never considered yourself ready.

For years I've hosted writing workshops and I've spoken at writing conferences because I understand the angst your desire has created. I'm pissed that I waited as long as I did to publish. My words aren't the best that have ever seen print, but hey, they're not the worst, either.

Let's agree that you, too, are somewhere in that same zone. Long gone are the days where some nameless, faceless person decrees your words *ready* for the masses. Screw them. Your words may sell just ten copies or they may sell millions. That's not up to some gatekeeper a thousand miles away. That's all on you.

As a hybrid author who has experienced both traditional and independent publishing, I love the opportunities that exist for writers today. You have choices. You can appeal to an agent who may or may not love you. That agent can submit your work to an editor who may or may not love you. That editor could sign you to a contract and publish your words to a public that may or may not love you.

Or you can do it all yourself and see what happens.

Sitting around and doing nothing, however, relegates you to the group of people who chose not to play the game at all. I don't know you, and I have no idea how well you write. Perhaps sitting out is for the best.

But I doubt it. You've already shown the curiosity it takes to step off the platform. Forget about the bullshit sales scorecard which intimidates so many.

You can hold a device in the palm of your hand that provides instant communication and lightning-fast access to information. I urge you to take advantage of that access, wherever you find it, then combine it with your creative spirit, and, at the very least, fulfill a desire you've incubated for so long.

Words can't describe how happy it will make you. You have ideas and dreams which are as valid and substantial as anyone's, and collectively they come in a vast palette of colors. John Lennon's advice was solid: *Listen to the color of your dreams.*

IT'S NICE TO SHARE

If this book has moved you, entertained you, and hopefully inspired you, I'm happy.

If you would encourage others with the same writing desire to pick up this book, I would be overjoyed. It's truly how writers survive: word of mouth and reviews.

Ah, yes. Reviews. If you'd be so kind to post one, it would mean a great deal to me.

Please share a link to the book's page at DomTesta.com, or any of the multiple online bookstores.

Thank you.

ABOUT MY WORDS

I've been fortunate in the writing world, with more than twenty published books. The first six comprised the *Galahad* series for young (and young-at-heart) adults. They were published by Tor/Macmillan, some of the best people you'll ever meet in this industry.

In 2019 I began writing a series of spy thrillers featuring a character named Eric Swan. As of late 2020, four of them have been published, and a fifth is in the works. (These are definitely *not* for kids.)

All of the info can be found at EricSwan.com, or at your favorite place to buy books.

My books for middle-grade students are under the pen name Buster Blank. Three of these weird books are in print so far, and a fourth has been almost finished for three years. No shit, three years. It's time I finished, since it's probably the best one.

The *Mindbender* books are fun for road trips, family gatherings, or I guess even as bathroom books. They've sold a bunch, and more are on the way.

There's also some creepy fiction written as Harlan Plumber. (See the anecdote in the chapter titled Inspire.)

Links to all of these titles are in the next section.

I walked into a radio station at age sixteen and asked for a job as a disc jockey. Somehow they said *sure*, and I've now been doing radio for more than forty years. It's still a total kick in the ass. Morning radio is (often) one of the greatest creative outlets in the world.

I also speak professionally on stage. I charge a lot, but I'm told it's worth every penny.

As for my personal life, I convinced a beautiful, talented, and funny woman to hang out with me. Don't ask me how. And I'm blessed to have the world's greatest son. He's a writer, too, and way better at it than I am. Bastard.

ALSO BY DOM TESTA

Writing As Dom Testa:

The Eric Swan Thriller series:

Power Trip: Eric Swan Thriller #1

Poison Control: Eric Swan Thriller #2

God Maker: Eric Swan Thriller #3

Field Agent: Eric Swan Thriller #4

The Galahad Series of Young Adult Sci-Fi

Galahad Archives Volume 1: Leaving Earth

(Contains two novels, *The Comet's Curse* and *The Web of Titan*)

Galahad Archives Volume 2: Into Deep Space

(Contains two novels, *The Cassini Code* and *The Dark Zone*)

Galahad Archives Volume 3: A New Life

(Contains two novels, *Cosmic Storm* and *The Galahad Legacy*)

The Mindbender Book Series (Games/Trivia)

The Mindbender Book, Volume 1

The Mindbender Book, Volume 2

The Mindbender Book, Volume 3

The Mindbender Book, Volume 4

The Mindbender Book, Volume 5

Writing As Buster Blank (for middle grade)

Shaking Demons

Madison Cooley's Shoes

My Favorite Nightmare

Writing As Harlan Plumber

Wednesday, and Other Dark Tales

Manufactured by Amazon.ca
Bolton, ON

19186155R00092